LIVING YOUR

A Survival Manual For People With Multiple Personalities

BY SANDRA J. HOCKING
AND COMPANY

being M.P.D. is an
always thing, from the
time [illegible] Hall etc Rachel
its been out in the open.
It doesn't make it any better
or easier to live with, others know
but don't understand

Launch Press

Rockville, MD

Printed in the United States of America

99 98 97 96 95 94 93 92 3 2 1

Library of Congress Cataloging-in-publicaton Data

Hocking, Sandra J., 1948-

Living with your selves : a survival manual for people with multiple personalities / by Sandra J. Hocking and company.

p. cm.

ISBN 1-877872-06-7 : $5.95

1. Multiple personality—Popular works. 2. Multiple personality—Treatment. I. Title.

RC569.5.M8H63 1992 92-16514

616.85'236—dc20 CIP

To my good friend
Linda Badeaux Sawyer

Without whose nimble fingers,
constant encouragement
and nagging

This book may never have been completed.

CONTENTS

FOREWORD

When Chris Sizemore, who is Eve of *The Three Faces of Eve*, was diagnosed in the 1950's, she was told that she was the only person on the planet with MPD. In 1979, when I saw my first case, there had been a total of about 200 cases of MPD reported in the world literature. My supervisors in medical school could not provide me with a single reference on MPD, and I had to do a hand search of the *Index Medicus* to build up a reference list for the paper I published on the case.

Today, studies indicate that MPD in fact affects about 1% of adults in the general population, and about 5% of general adult psychiatric inpatients. The dissociative disorder as a group appear to be about as common as the anxiety and mood disorders, and a bit less common than substance abuse: about 10% of the general population has had a dissociative disorder at some time in their lives.

This means that several million people with MPD in North America might benefit from reading *Living With Your Selves*.

Besides being relatively common, MPD is often highly treatable. As Sandra Hocking points out, the goal of treatment may be integration or cooperative function based on negotiation between non-integrated alters. Her idea of joining is an original contribution to the literature and adds a subtle modification to the previously described outcomes. Whether integrated or not, the successfully treated person with MPD experiences a dramatic improvement in function, and much reduced pain and systems, and can enter into much healthier relationships.

Research on the economic cost-benefit of the diagnosis and treatment of MPD in Canada indicates that making the diagnosis and providing the treatment could save as much as $250,000.00 per case compared to the cost of years of incorrect diagnoses, ineffective treatments, and repeated hospitalization. Not everyone with MPD requires hospitalization, but many do.

Living With Your Selves is the first self-help manual for MPD. The fact that it is written by someone with MPD is evident throughout, in that this is an insider's view, and written from the heart. At the same time, the manual is balanced and sensible, and reviews the diagnosis and treatment of MPD accurately and in detail. Few mental health professionals currently in training will emerge from their studies with this comprehensive an understanding of MPD!

Although the manual is written for people with MPD, it should also be read by mental health professionals, and friends and family of persons with MPD. As well, the manual would be very helpful for the large number of people who have partial and incomplete forms of MPD, referred to in the psychiatric literature as dissociative disorder not otherwise specified, of DDNOS. I suspect that DDNOS probably affects 2-5% of the general population and at least 10% of people treated by psychiatrists.

MPD has more to teach us abut the human mind, and how human beings cope with trauma, than any other diagnosis. MPD is not strange, weird, bizarre or incomprehensible: it is the characteristic human response to severe, chronic childhood trauma. Sandra Hocking has embodied this truth beautifully in her manual. What the person with MPD has done to survive severe trauma, everyone does to a lesser degree in life. I believe that MPD will teach us a great deal about normal, healthy multiplicity and will help correct an error our culture has made in its basic philosophy of the self.

Having alter personalities who try to kill each other, are amnesic for each other, and carry huge amounts of unresolved trauma, is not normal or healthy. But it is not really the multiplicity that is the problem with MPD: rather it is the conflict, self-destructiveness, abnormal amnesia, and abnormal personification of the part-selves. All systems, including the human mind, are composed of subsystems, and it is normal for these subsystems to function fairly independently at times. MPD can teach us a great deal about all of this, if we listen. Sandra Hocking is one of those we should listen to.

Colin A. Ross, M.D.

Acknowledgements

No book is ever written alone. I owe many thanks to the following people, who helped, supported, and loved me. They believed in this book, and in me.

Robert J. Grosch, M.Div., M.A., my therapist, planted the idea for the book, read the first draft, and made constructive suggestions.

Linda Badeaux Sawyer, spent many long hours on the manuscript, typing, editing, and polishing. I am also grateful to Laura Miller, who did the final editing.

Drew Sawyer, Linda's husband, accepted me and supported the project, even as I took over their house and disrupted their schedules while the book was in progress.

Chip Hocking, my husband, has had to put up with me for twelve years. This man deserves the Congressional Medal of Honor, as I am no peach to live with! Without his support, kindness, safety, stability, and love, I might not have survived to write a book.

Some friends read the manuscript and made suggestions or simply believed in me: Liz Davis, Michelle Young, Cristi Williams, Claudia Hotchkiss, Sydney Lockett, Susie Boone, Larry Licker, Jack Rasmussen, Barbara Heater, and Jay and Kathy Skender.

Mary Banvard is one of the finest singletons I know. When all I could see was confusion, she steadfastly kept showing me my health.

Thanks to the members of the old MPD group. I don't know where you are, or what you are doing, but I hope all is well with you. You helped me more than you know.

These counselors saw me through the hard times: Ellen Bass, Amy Pine, Vic and Sue Harwood, Barbara Henderson, Bob Buley, and Quentin Henley.

And last, but certainly not least, I owe a debt of gratitude to John Lynch, Publisher of Launch Press, and to Dr. Eliana Gil, for "loving my book!"

Introduction

There may be any number of reasons why you are reading this book. Your therapist may have told you that you have multiple personalities. You may suspect you have multiple personalities, and are reading this book for confirmation. You may be a clinician or counselor who needs more information. You may have a friend or loved one who is a multiple.

In any case, and whoever you are, welcome.

This is not a clinical textbook. It was written by a multiple, for other multiples. This book is designed to help those with multiple personalities and other dissociative states live with their condition. Notice I said "condition" and not "disorder." Having multiple personalities does not have to be a disorder. The development of multiple personalities is a highly creative defense mechanism that, when accepted and understood, can be made to work for you rather than against you.

This is meant to be a practical book. The language is deliberately kept simple so that the younger members of your internal system can understand it. In general, I'll be talking to your "host personality" (the one who spends most of the time living in the world), with the understanding that some of the "others" (called alters) will be reading over your shoulder. I have avoided using clinical terms as much as possible, and will explain terms as we go along.

This book will ask a number of questions. Any answers I provide come from my own experience, research and realm of understanding. (I don't discuss hospitalization, for example, because I have not had that experience.) As I said, this is not a clinical book. This is a survivor's book.

Today, many survivors have shared their stories with the world. That's great! Acknowledging one's multiplicity is a courageous and powerful act. Disclosures of trauma that cause multiple personalities are validating and helpful to other survivors. The stories provide identification, show proof that this condition actually exists, and help relieve feelings of isolation.

When I first realized I was a multiple, I looked for a book that could help me live with my condition. There wasn't one. I told my therapist I wanted my story, my experience, my pain to count for something. I wanted other survivors to know they could heal. I wanted a "how-to manual" for living. I wanted to help. My therapist, Robert J. Grosch, M. Div., M. A. (hereafter referred to as Bob), suggested "the book that hasn't been written yet. How to live with multiple personalities, not just how you got it in the first place." I liked that idea, so I wrote this book to fill in the gap between the clinical literature and survivors' stories.

If there is one thing I hope you glean from this book, it's that having multiple personalities is not something to be feared. Multiplicity is what helped me survive, and it has helped you, too. I hope this book can give you some skills to live with your condition, and the confidence that you can.

From All of Us,

To All of You,

Sandra J. Hocking

And Company

Chapter One

Multiplicity Is . . .

What does it mean to have multiple personalities?

Well, imagine a bus, with the "host" or main personality as the bus itself. Inside the bus, passengers are sleeping, reading, playing, or looking out different windows. Sometimes a passenger will climb into the driver's seat to direct where the bus goes and what it does, often without the bus's knowledge or consent. (This process of changing drivers is called "switching.")

All that most people know about multiple personalities is what they read in a book or see in the movies. They see Sybil standing in ponds and crawling up bookshelves, or Eve (*The Three Faces of Eve*) trying to strangle her small daughter. They see Truddi Chase (*When Rabbit Howls*) holed up in an abandoned warehouse or shoving a census taker down the stairs. They see the Boston Strangler killing women in their homes.

It's no wonder the public is afraid.

What they don't see are the many multiples who have homes, families, jobs, and who live a fairly normal life. It doesn't make good copy. It doesn't make money. It's not dramatic.

People with multiple personalities have a psychiatric condition that is caused by severe childhood trauma such as rape, incest, physical torture, or ritualistic abuse, sometimes at the hands of a satanic cult. It is a condition of having two or more separate persons or personalities who inhabit the same body, and at least two of these persons or personalities take control of the person's behavior. Multiplicity is a highly creative and effective method of dealing with pain, trauma, fear and often life-threatening situations.

It is not demonic possession!

To defend against fear, dissociation techniques are learned in childhood. Dissociation is the normal ability to "leave" the body in stressful or boring situations. Everybody dissociates. Daydreaming, highway hypnosis and simple "spacing out" are examples of dissociation. Multiples, however, take "normal" dissociation to a different level, one in which the "self" seems to disappear, or "leaves," and other "selves" take over to handle a variety of situations.

Multiples live complicated lives. Alternate personalities (alters) may come "out" at inopportune moments and disrupt a conversation. Time loss can be frequent, severe and frightening.

Most multiples live in fear that someone will find out they are multiples, and they will lose their job or family. Traditional churches may attempt to "exorcise the demons that possess" the multiple. Friends, frightened of the unknown, may disappear.

Unfortunately, many multiples are left to the care of therapists who are uninformed or disbelieving. Others find therapists who have taken the time and trouble to become trained and capable in treating this condition. This can mean the difference between life and death for the multiple.

Let's talk for a minute about accepting the diagnosis of having multiple personalities. Part of being a multiple is constantly questioning your own perceptions and your own reality. You may be presented with absolute, irrefutable evidence of your multiplicity and still doubt that you're a multiple. This is a normal part of the process. You can believe it one minute and totally reject it the next. Especially, I think, if your multiplicity is on the milder end of the scale. It's common to watch the movies and read the dramatic literature and think your own manifestation of this condition is not real.

Acceptance of the diagnosis will be an ongoing part of your therapy.

Chapter Two

My Story

I would like to tell you something about me. I will share some of my history with you, as well as the discovery of my multiplicity and what my life is like today.

When I was about six months old, my Uncle Dan , who was also busy molesting the rest of my siblings, stuck his penis down my throat. I almost choked to death on his semen. This initial abuse set the stage for the first "split." A split occurs when trauma experienced is too much for the psyche to bear, and an existing or new personality comes out to take the pain or handle the situation. Uncle Dan also molested my brother Bobby, who later became my main tormentor.

From the time I was three years old, Bobby tortured, abused and raped me. I believe he penetrated me for the first time when I was three. I came home, with blood running down my leg, only to be yelled at by my mother for "sticking things inside" me. She washed me and sent me back out to play. By this time, I had already learned to compartmentalize the abuse into other personalities. With this penetration, "Shasha" was created.

When I was about three or four, we went to visit an uncle who lived on a ranch. During this visit, I was taken into the barn by my brother and some of his friends, stripped naked, tied up, and raped by them and with foreign objects. I had many splits during this time.

Also during this period, Bobby decided to play "Hitler," and put me in the oven. Aaron was created to protect me. I was locked in a toy box and left; Amanda was created. We lived in a motel for a while, where I met a little girl. What I now suspect was natural sexual exploration was too threatening for my fragile self, and Liz (the lesbian in my system) was created.

At some point between the ages of three and six, we lived next to someone involved with a satanic cult. This cult was comprised of women witches. The abuse took the form of physical and sexual torture, watching human sacrifice, cannibalism and bestiality. Much of the ritual abuse memories are still buried. (I am hesitant to name them here, not because of fear of reprisal, but because I don't want you to fill in your own empty places with my memories.) At least four of my alters were created during this time. Luckily, we did not live there for long, but unluckily, the torture that my brother learned at the hands of the cult was carried on when we left.

Bobby continued to abuse me until I was thirteen, when he went into the service. By this time I was highly fragmented. However, with the danger from Bobby past, the alters who were created to protect me went underground. "I" went on to live my life.

I became very promiscuous, going from man to man to man, looking for love and affection wherever I could find it. . . abusive men, alcoholics and emotional batterers. It was all I knew, and all I thought I deserved. I sold my body, and Regina came to be.

When I was thirty years old, after two children and two divorces, I met my current husband. I was finally in a safe environment, with a man who did not abuse me. Life continued.

I had always used compulsive eating as a defense mechanism, using food to stuff down feelings and memories, even though I had long since buried the memories of abuse. If you had asked me, I would have told you that I had had a normal, albeit adventurous childhood. Finally, I decided to do something about my weight, and joined a twelve-step program to deal with it. Two years into abstinence from compulsive eating, the weight came off. . . and the memories began.

I had my first flashback when I was thirty-eight. I was sitting on my bed at the age of eleven or so, with Bobby standing in front of me with an erect penis. The flashback terrified me. I went running into therapy, horrified that I would think such a thing, terrified that it might be true, and even more terrified that I might be making it all up. Incest memories surfaced. The journey had begun.

About one year into therapy, I went to a psychodrama workshop in Portland, Oregon. When it came my turn to work, I became so stressed that one of my alters, Millie, came out. I receded into the background, and I was outside my body looking in at the scene. When I came home from the workshop, I told Bob what had happened. He wasn't particularly surprised.

After Millie, the others began to make themselves known. More and more kept coming. I felt crazier and crazier. I must be making this up, I thought. Surely this couldn't be true. But the alters and memories kept coming. It took a long time, but as I began to know these other parts of myself, I began to accept them, and be grateful to them for saving me from death and insanity.

Today, I'm still married to my safe and supportive husband. Until recently, I worked at a women's refuge, where I counselled victims of domestic violence and sexual assault. I facilitated two support groups for sexual assault survivors. I supervised twenty rape crisis advocates and was responsible for their initial and ongoing training. I made numerous community outreach presentations, including radio and television. I was in charge of my agency's child assault prevention program, and supervised the coordinator and facilitators. In addition, it was my responsibility to be sure all the statistics needed for our grant money was kept accurate and up-to-date.

Currently, I am self-employed as an educator and consultant to women's shelters, schools and law enforcement. I still make community outreach presentations and speak at child abuse conferences.

I write (obviously), and enjoy bowling, poetry, and hiking. My life is more normal than it ever has been. And yet, I'm still a multiple. My alters still take control sometimes, and stand ready to protect me if necessary. They always give me input into the circumstances of my life. We cooperate well together.

My life as a multiple is often complicated, and sometimes scary, sad and lonely. It is also rewarding, fulfilling and humorous. Life, after all, is never a flat line, but a series of peaks and valleys.

I imagine yours is, too.

Chapter Three

Signs & Symptoms Of Multiple Personality

Recognition of multiple personalities is simple, yet it is often misdiagnosed. Look over the definition in the chapter on terminology to see how a therapist arrives at the diagnosis.

As you read through the following signs and symptoms and if you find yourself saying, "Yes, yes, uh-huh, oh! that, too!" to most of the questions, then you might be a multiple. If you recognize yourself here, hotfoot it to your therapist and say, "Look at this! This is me!" and go on from there.

Here are some signs to look for:

1. How much of your childhood do you remember? Do you have long periods of time, years perhaps, you can't recall? Amnesia of childhood memories alone does not a multiple make. Lots of survivors block out painful episodes from their childhoods, but that doesn't mean they are multiples. Amnesia alone is not a clear indicator of multiplicity, but if it exists with other symptoms, then it becomes a possibility.

2. How much of your adult life can you remember? Do you remember yesterday? Last week? Last year? Only bits and pieces? Do you remember what you had for dinner a week ago last Tuesday? (Neither does my friend Mary, but she doesn't have multiple personalities. Some things are just not important enough to remember. Don't go overboard

with this.) If you find yourself "coming to" in various situations, with no idea how you got there, you may have multiple personalities.

Do you have periods during the day when you just can't remember what went on before? The last thing you remember it was ten o'clock in the morning, and now it's four o'clock in the afternoon, and you don't know what went on between ten and four? Time loss can be a sign of multiplicity.

Has time always been a very scary thing for you? Do you find yourself looking at your watch in order to judge your last conscious memory?

3. Do you hear voices? Do you hear conversations going on inside your head, in different voices? Is there a running commentary going on inside most of the time? Do you sleep with music on to drown out the voices?

When I hear my voices, it sounds like somebody turned on a radio full blast in my head. I startle, and my heart starts pounding about a hundred miles an hour. Before I knew what it was, I would think: "What the heck is that?" Now that I'm aware of what's happening, the startle reflex has diminished considerably.

Where do your voices come from? Are they inside your head, or outside? If you talk to the lamp post, and the lamp post talks back, that's not a sign of multiplicity, but could be serious. If the voices are inside your head, though, that is one indicator of multiple personalities. Talk to a mental health professional about any voices you hear.

By the way, singletons (people with one or fewer personalities!) don't hear voices. Oh, sure, they think and reason with themselves, but they don't hear voices. I never knew that. I've heard my voices for so long, I thought it was "normal."

4. Do you open your mouth in a restaurant, and hear yourself order something you know you hate? For example,

I hate sauerkraut. One day at lunch, fully expecting to order a cheeseburger, I opened my mouth and the words that came out were, "I'll have a Reuben sandwich!" Liz is the one who likes sauerkraut, so I "left" while she ate lunch. When Liz was finished with her Reuben, "I" came back and ordered my cheeseburger, much to the astonishment of the waitress!

Do you say things you have no intention of saying? Like, "Is that a new toupee?" to your husband's boss.

Do you do things you have no intention of doing? One morning I set out for a short little drive to the coast, and ended up in Reno, four hours in the opposite direction!

5. Do you find yourself driving the car, and for a moment (or several) not know where you came from or where you're going? Now, I'm not talking about the common form of dissociation called "highway hypnosis" that even singletons get. This is a more complete "arrival," with little or no knowledge of what went on before.

6. Do you often feel removed or distant from your surroundings, like you are watching yourself? As you watch, are you aware that you couldn't change a single word or action, even if you tried? Do you start writing, and the words just appear on the paper, without any conscious thought on your part?

I believe that being "influenced" from the inside is a much more common manifestation of multiplicity than clear and complete switching. It feels like being controlled from the inside, as though you were only a vehicle for somebody else's behavior. At one point, one alter had control of my thoughts, somebody else had my mouth, and still another had control of my body. It was a frightening time.

7. Have you made the rounds of therapist after therapist, being treated for everything from schizophrenia to borderline personality disorder, given drugs, sent to

hospitals, and nobody can seem to find out what's wrong with you? It sometimes takes years for an accurate diagnosis of multiplicity to be made. That's getting better, though, as more clinicians are being trained in the diagnosis and treatment of this condition.

8. Do medications work on you in different ways, with each dose? Sometimes the dose seems too strong and sometimes not strong enough? Can you be ill with a cold, and an hour later be perfectly healthy?

9. Do you suddenly "come to" and find that it's an hour, day, month, or year from the last time you remember being "there?" Have you spent a lot of time and energy covering up for things you couldn't remember? Did your teachers tell you "What's wrong with you? You knew this material backwards and forwards yesterday." The problem is, you've never seen this stuff before in your life.

10. Do you find clothes, books, cigarettes, alcohol or food you know you didn't buy? Do strange charges appear on your credit card bills from pornography shops, hardware stores or other places you never go? Are you constantly in debt because you've bought things you don't remember buying? Do you get magazines and catalog items in the mail you don't remember ordering? Do you find liquor containers in the trash, but you don't drink?

Do you have wigs in various styles, lengths and colors that you don't recall either buying or wearing? Do people tell you that you have a twin in town, but that the person looks and acts differently than you do?

11. Do you write in more than one handwriting? Even singletons have a neat hand and a sloppy one, a fast hand and a careful one. I'm talking about truly different handwritings. Some look like childish scrawls, others proper and controlled. Others may look like chicken scratch, and yet another may be full of curly-cues. Some of the writing may be very tiny, while some is large and flamboyant. The pressure of the writing may change with

each author, or the slant may be different. If you do this, you know what I mean.

12. Are you drawn to teddy bears, dolls, coloring books, and bright, shiny, toy fire engines? Most multiples have at least one "inner" child, and have houses filled with kids' toys, even if they have no children of their own.

13. Do you avoid mirrors? You may not find this one in the clinical books, but many multiples avoid mirrors like the plague. The face you expect is never quite the face you get, and it's more than a little disconcerting to see somebody else's face reflected back at you.

Clinicians will tell you that the face actually appears to change when the client switches from one personality to another. For example, a child alter may seem younger, more innocent; the cheekbones may appear higher or the lips fuller. Sometimes even the drape of the hair appears to change.

14. Do you have absolutely no concept of your body size? Does your body seem to feel or look a different size from day to day? Are you certain that you wear a size 12, only to find that a 10 or a 14 fits? Do you have a closet full of clothes in varying sizes, styles and colors? (I have some clothes in my closet that I wouldn't be caught dead at a dog fight in, but somebody in the system likes them.) Do you own hats that you know "you" never wear?

15. Do you have to readjust the seat and mirror every time you get in the car, even though you're the only one who drives that car? Or do you find the gas level changes from day to day, even if you haven't gone anywhere?

16. When doctors and therapists ask you questions, do you answer "I don't know. I can't remember. I've always had a terrible memory." Do you really have a terrible memory or is it that you can't remember? Having a terrible memory and not being able to remember because you were "somebody else" are two very different things.

17. If you're a female, do you almost always wear pants? Do you sometimes have a real aversion to feminine clothes? Do you hate to wear a bra? The males in my system won't come out if "we" are wearing a dress. (One of my protectors is male, so he feels his hands are tied if I'm in danger, and I'm dressed in a feminine way.)

If you're a male, are you sometimes drawn to women's clothing? Have you ever found yourself wearing clothing of the opposite sex, and not remembered either buying it, or putting it on?

18. Are significant events in your life a blank? Things like getting married, graduating, doing military service, or having a baby? You know you did these things, because you see proof before you, but you don't really remember them.

19. Do people accuse you of lying? This is something multiples have lived with their whole life. People say they saw you do something you have no memory of doing, or they have to remind you of conversations you don't remember having. Again, this is not the common distracted inattention of singletons, but evidence of time loss.

20. Can you give a clear step-by-step, year-by-year description of where you lived as a child, what the inside of your house looked like, where you went to school or who your teachers and best friends were? If the answer to this is no, you're not alone. Many multiples can't remember these things either, but just not being able to remember doesn't necessarily mean you're a multiple. Look at the whole picture.

21. Do you have flashbacks or nightmares? Do you find yourself in the produce section of the supermarket, looking at the cucumbers, and suddenly you're in the bedroom and you're nine years old and your father is looking at you and . . . Do you have nightmares regularly — sometimes two, three or more a night? Do you wonder if the nightmares are dreams, or memories?

Nightmares and flashbacks are two different things, by the way. A nightmare happens while you're asleep. A flashback is an intrusive memory that happens when you're awake.

Once again, you need to be careful. Nightmares and flashbacks alone are not indicative of multiplicity.

22. Do you wake up in the morning and find evidence that you've been busy during the night? Writings, art work, furniture rearranged? Or have you acquired a talent you don't remember learning? How to play the flute, how to paint, how to type?

23. Do you find yourself talking in voices that don't seem to belong to you? For example, when I told my brother Billy I was a multiple, his first response was, "Oh, is that what happens when you talk baby talk?" "I don't talk baby talk!" I exclaimed. "Sure, you do," he said, "all the time."

Do people ask you where your accent went? One of my alters, Marta, has an unmistakable Yorkshire accent. When she talks, people listen!

24. Do you often say "we," "he," or "she" instead of "I" or "me?" One of the first clues Bob had that I was a multiple was that I seemed to be referring to other people when I was talking about myself. This came out in my writing as well.

25. Do you injure yourself without knowing how, when or why? Do you find cuts, burns, scratches or bruises on your body that you can't explain? Do you find evidence that some destructive force has been loose, but you have no memory of it?

Many survivors, multiples or not, experience what are called "body memories," in which the body itself retains, feels and displays the effects of abuse. It's sometimes difficult to tell the difference between a body memory and being injured in the present by a destructive alter.

26. Are you a survivor of ritual abuse? When an adult or child is abused in a ritualized manner, we use the term 'ritual abuse.' It is a systematic and organized form of abuse that uses severe sexual, physical, emotional and spiritual torture to gain control over a person. It may involve many perpetrators and many victims. The abuse may be done as part of a satanic or occult ritual; as part of an organized fundamental belief system; by a group of "dabblers;" or sometimes by a single individual. Not all ritual abuse is satanic, but ritual abuse includes abuse done during satanic rituals.

Clinical literature suggests that many survivors of ritual abuse are multiples. The kind of abuse that happens at the hands of a cult or coven is horrendous, so it is quite common to find multiplicity among ritual abuse survivors.

Just because you're a multiple does not necessarily mean that ritual abuse was part of your experience. Conversely, if you are a ritual abuse survivor, you don't necessarily have to be a multiple. As you work in therapy, it will become clear whether ritual abuse is part of your history.

27. Has your therapist told you that you have multiple personalities? Although many therapists are unwilling to consider the diagnosis of multiple personalities except as a last resort, some use the diagnosis as a "more is better" approach. Your therapist may make the diagnosis of multiplicity simply because you talk about amnesia for childhood events, losing time, or your "inner children."

As you work in therapy, however, it will become clear if this diagnosis fits for you.

So. You've read through the list and found yourself saying, "Yes, yes, uh-huh and oh! that, too!" Now what?

Read on. That's what the rest of the book is all about – how to live with multiple personalities.

Chapter Four

Meeting Your Selves

Meeting your other selves can be frightening, exciting, painful and joyous. You may find some who you like a lot, others that scare you. You may have alters who are talented and sophisticated, others who are autistic, silent, or fragmented. You may discover alters who are destructive or who act in sexually inappropriate ways. You're almost guaranteed to have children in your system, as well as protectors and persecutors.

The most important thing to remember is that every one of your inside people helped you survive. They are what enabled you to read this book today. Even if you don't think you like them very much right now, they are your friends. They're a part of you, and you've been together for a long, long time. You've made one heck of a journey together. And you've all got a lot of work to do now.

You may have alters who seem like full-fledged "people," and alters who are fragments, who only hold a memory or two, or who only perform a specific function.

I want to talk about some of the alters you may have in your system, which means that I'm going to talk about my own people. You may or may not have similar folks. Bob tells me I'm pretty "typical" (whatever that means), so I'm just going to have to assume that your system is similar in some respects to mine. I call my alters "people" and I've heard other multiples call their alters "parts" or "inside people."

I have thirty-seven people living in this body. You may have more or you may have less. The number of people you have is not important. What is important is that everybody in the system is vital, every single one of you.

THE KIDS

It's probably easiest to start with the children in the system. Your kids may be any age and many ages. You may have infants, toddlers, older kids and teenagers. Each one carries a piece of your past, a bit of your memory, and a lot of strength and courage.

Child alters create their own special situations. It can be very embarrassing when a little one comes out at the toy store and says "I want a dolly!" and throws a heel-kicking tantrum on the floor. But the joy of watching a child alter blossom in the sunshine of a safe relationship is very rewarding.

You didn't become a multiple by living in Beaver Cleaver's house, and you're not a member of the Brady Bunch, either. You developed multiple personalities because you were hurt very badly as a child. Those children who live inside you are the ones who carry the hurt, the pain, the terror and the memories.

Go to a playground or school sometime and watch the kids. See what an eight-year-old girl looks, acts and plays like. See how a four-year-old boy talks. Notice how small these children are. That's you, some years ago. Small. Trusting. Innocent. Powerless.

Your alters (kids and adults) tend to group together according to the kind of abuse they suffered, or by the function they serve. In my system, children Margret, Twelve, Betsy, and Brave lived through the ritual abuse, and these kids hurt a lot. Adults Marta, Jessica, and Liz protect the children, as does Millie, who is little more than a child herself. Kate, Roberta and I go to work.

You and your therapist will probably work with your inside kids a great deal. As scary and painful as the memories are, it is important they get a chance to come out and work through these experiences. They need to share what happened to them with you and with the rest of your system so that everyone can heal.

However, flashbacks and memories don't always happen in the relative safety of your therapist's office. Sometimes they happen at home, and sometimes they happen in public. It's important to have a safety plan in place beforehand.

If you feel a memory coming on, get to a safe place. If you're at work, go home. If you're out in public, try to get to your car. The best place, of course, is home, if that is where you feel the safest. If you think you will need a support person with you, call someone who will know how to deal with you and your alters. Call your therapist, if that seems appropriate. If you have child alters who are destructive, you can ask the protectors to be nearby to safeguard the system.

If you can't get to a safe place right away, it's important to acknowledge the memory, then put it aside until you can deal with it. This means that you mentally recognize the memory, internally explain that you are unable to address it now and make a commitment to yourself and your alters to deal with it later. It's very important to keep the commitment and follow up. This takes work, practice and cooperation between your selves, but it can be done.

Inner children who are destructive, either to themselves, others, or property, are trying to get your attention. They're hurting very badly. If they are destructive, it's because they're calling out for help. They're trying to tell, in spite of all the warnings and threats to keep silent.

There are some things you can do to help them. Provide a safe place for them to deal with their memories. That means a place in your home that you've "child-proofed." Yep, just like you would with young children. Pad the sharp corners of tables. Keep objects that cut or burn safely out of reach. Provide lots of pillows to pound on and cuddly animals, teddy bears, or dolls to hold. Supply crayons and paper so the non-verbal kids will have a way to process their pain.

You may also have children who were designed simply to have fun and play. I have a few in my system. Twins Misty and Monica just get to be kids. Don't fight it! Let them out to play! Go to the park. Swing on the swing sets. Play on the monkey bars or in the sand. It's okay to have fun. Go see a Disney movie, or better yet, rent one to see at home. Buy a set of Tinker Toys or Lincoln Logs. Keep Play-Dough around. When you're in the store and find yourself being drawn to a toy or doll, that's one of your inner kids talking. Go ahead, give in and buy it. Your inside kids have been deprived of a normal, happy childhood. It's okay for you to help them have it now.

SEXUAL ALTERS

You may have some alters in your system who act in sexually inappropriate ways. If you're a multiple, most likely you were sexually abused as a child, so sexual "acting out" is almost to be expected. For many of these alters, sex is the only thing they feel they are good for, or good at. When you've been sexualized so early, it's easy to continue the pattern.

If you have an alter who insists on having sex with either a variety of partners or "undesirables," buy some condoms, and try to contract so s/he agrees to use them.

You may also have alters who want absolutely nothing to do with sex. It's important they understand that they have the choice to abstain. If you're in a relationship, and wish to have sexual relations with your partner, let the others know it's okay to disappear for a while. Your alters can be taught to remove themselves from stressful or uncomfortable situations. I just tell the children that I'm a big person and I can take care of them. I tell them it's okay for them to leave. I usually ask Millie to watch them for a while in her room, or for Marta to entertain them for a while. The adults in my system are not interested in having sex with my husband, so that makes life a lot easier for me! They just "go away" on their own accord.

If you were ritualistically abused as a child, you may have an alter whose function it was to have sex with animals. You may wish to reconsider having pets at this time. Unless you have a very cooperative system, and can be assured that your pets will be safe (and your alters won't feel the need to reenact this scenario), it may be best to forego animals right now. If you do have pets, and just can't bear to part with them, it's very important that you contract with the protectors in your system to protect you, your alters, and your pets.

You may have people in your system who are the opposite gender as yourself. That's okay! I have some males in my system. Aaron is a frightened young child, while Peter is adventurous and isn't afraid of anything. I have an adult male protector as well. You may have a male alter who is mechanically inclined, which makes him handy to have around.

It's important to remember that even singletons are a bit of both male and female. We just have a more distinct split than they do. Allow your opposite-gender alters expression, just as you allow all your others expression. They're important, too.

If you're married and some of your people aren't married to your spouse, you may have to do some heavy-duty contracting. Some of your children may see your spouse as a parent figure, or as a threat; the adolescents might prefer to form additional relationships; and gay or lesbian alters present their own set of challenges.

Complicated? You betcha!

That's where communication becomes a vital part of keeping the system safe and stable.

If you have alters who are acting in sexual ways that are not to your liking, they are doing it for any number of reasons and part of good therapy is finding out what those reasons are and reaching a useful compromise.

PERSECUTORS, SUICIDAL ALTERS AND ALTERS WHO INJURE THEMSELVES

People injure themselves in a variety of ways, and for a variety of reasons. Cutting or burning yourself, sticking needles in your arm, raking your fingernails across your skin, or pulling out your hair are all forms of self-injury. So is chain-smoking, doing drugs and compulsive overeating. Not all self-injury is meant to kill or maim.

If you have alters who are injuring themselves or attempting suicide, view that as a serious cry for help. Don't sluff it off and don't try to hide it. It's absolutely vital that your therapist know because s/he can't help you unless s/he knows what's going on.

ALTERS WHO INJURE THE BODY

Sometimes there is so much pain inside, cutting or burning seems like a release. At least you can put a bandage on the injury. Emotional pain is more shadowy, more nebulous, like trying to hold on to a cloud. You know the pain is there, but you can't get a firm grip on it.

It can prove to yourself that you are still alive and can still feel; it's a way of saying, "Look at me! Can't you see how much pain I'm in?! Help me!"

Injuring oneself may be a way of trying to pluck out the "offending" parts of the body. Sometimes alters who are of the opposite gender may attempt crude surgery on themselves to match the gender they feel they are.

Ritual abuse survivors may feel the urge to injure or destroy themselves in response to programming from the cult. They are programmed that if they tell, they'll die, so the injury or suicide attempts become programmed responses.

Programming and brainwashing are terms that are frightening for survivors. They seem to convey helplessness and powerlessness. In reality, programming and brainwashing are simply posthypnotic suggestions which can be successfully diffused in therapy.

If you are injuring yourself, first of all, tell your therapist! Your therapist can help you discover why you want to hurt yourself and help you to stop. You don't have to hurt yourself anymore! The people who hurt you when you were a kid were wrong and they did bad things to you. They may have told you that you deserved to be hurt, but they lied. You don't deserve to be hurt any more.

If you haven't injured yourself yet, but are thinking about it, tell your therapist! Yes, I know I sound like a broken record, but there are some subjects that a book just can't do justice to, and this is one of them. You can contract with your protectors, and you can keep sharp and burning objects out of reach to a certain extent, but that won't solve the problem. Good therapy, on the other hand, can reduce or eliminate these destructive urges as you get to the root causes of them.

People who injure themselves will tell you that after a while it becomes an obsessive/compulsive behavior that they have precious little control over. If you haven't started yet, don't. If you are currently injuring yourself, work on it in therapy, even though it may be scary to talk about.

Every time you hurt yourself, you hurt everybody inside you as well. Every time you take drugs or drink alcohol or smoke cigarettes, you destroy a bit more of the body you all share. Every time you cut yourself, burn yourself, or do damage to your body or soul, your abusers win another round. Fight back! Don't let the abusers win again!

SUICIDAL ALTERS

If you have alters that are suicidal, you may be in serious danger. Tell your therapist!

The good news is you're still alive and you're reading this today. Which means that in addition to the persecutors in your system, you have at least one protector as well. These are the folks who have kept you from serious harm in the past, and will continue to do so, given half a chance.

Just like those who injure themselves, suicidal alters are in a lot of pain. I can't stop you from killing yourself. Ultimately every choice is your choice. But, so many of us have died. From the abuse itself, from suicide, from cult programming. Your abusers violated your body and split your soul into pieces. Don't let them kill you, too.

I know how much this hurts. I know that sometimes it seems like the only way out is to end it all. I know how it is when every memory is worse than the one before, and what it's like to rack up abusers like beads on an abacus. I know the betrayal by the very people who were supposed to love and protect you. I know what it's like to stand at the kitchen sink for hours with the knife in your hand, wondering if this time you'll really do it. I know. I know.

But, my God. Life. Life is out there. Life is in here! Life is the trees and the grass and the flowers. Life is seeing my daughters grow up, and friends who love me. Life is playing with my dogs after work, and eating cheeseburgers or chocolate covered cherries. It's holding the fresh innocence of a newborn baby. Life is wondering what tomorrow brings, and then being there to find out. Life is writing this book, opening up the pages of my life.

I didn't split into thirty-seven different people in order to survive just so I could kill us all later. Please. Don't let them kill you. It gets better. Honest to God, it does.

And sometimes, just living is the best revenge.

Chapter Five

Choosing A Therapist

This chapter is mostly for people who don't have a therapist yet, though it should be helpful for others as well.

Let's say that you suspect you're a multiple. You've read everything you can get your hands on, and everything fits. Multiplicity explains too much of your life for it not to be true. So you go to your therapist, and s/he says, "There is no such thing as multiple personalities." Now what? Whether or not you choose to stay is up to you, of course, but if you're being treated for something you don't have, and not being treated for something you do, then you're not getting the best care possible. You should not, however, try to diagnose yourself. So you may wish to explore this question more fully before moving on to another therapist.

Choosing a therapist is not easy. Therapists come in all shapes, sizes, sexes and levels of competence. Some are great and some are not so great. Some are conservative and some are innovative. Some are "touchers" and some aren't. Some "believe" in multiple personalities, and some don't. You need one who does.

There are a few things to remember when shopping for a therapist. One is that you have the right to make choices and mistakes. This means you have the right to change therapists if you're not getting what you need. You have the right to be treated with respect, even if you've done something dumb, destructive, or inappropriate. You have the right to control the pace and intensity of your therapy.

I deliberately use the phrase 'shopping for a therapist' because that's exactly what you're doing. The therapist is selling his or her services, and you are buying them. You have a right to your money's worth.

Therapy can be an expensive proposition. Insurance helps. But even if you have no insurance or financial help of any kind, you still need an individual therapist if you have multiple personalities. Bottom line. Cut down on cigarettes and beer (better yet, cut them out), spend a little less on potato chips and ice cream.

This is important! This is your life we're talking about here. A competent, caring therapist is not a luxury, but an absolute necessity. And yes, you're worth it. If you don't get therapy, if you don't get help, then the people who hurt you win again. It's time we survivors won, for a change!

Okay, so, let's shop.

The first place to start looking for a good therapist is not in the Yellow Pages. You can't choose a therapist by potluck because you like the name, or the location of the office, or because their fee is lower, or they accept your brand of insurance.

The first place to start looking is by asking around. That doesn't mean asking the clerk at the five-and-dime. Ask your doctor for a referral. Then, talk with your best friend and say, "You know, I've been thinking about getting some counselling. Have you heard of any good therapists in this area?" Listen to what s/he says. Ask a lot of people. Listen to a lot of answers. Your head may reel, but after a while a pattern will begin to emerge. The same name will keep cropping up (either good or bad).

Next, call your local rape crisis hotline or local child abuse prevention council. Ask for a referral. Many of these organizations have a list of therapists they have interviewed for appropriateness and skill.

Then call your state's licensing agency who will respond to questions regarding specific therapists. The agency can tell you if a therapist has had their license suspended or revoked, or if it is under investigation. Obviously, avoid these people.

Okay, so the same name keeps coming up, and you've decided to take the plunge and call Sally Smith, marriage, family, child counselor (MFCC, for short). And no, you don't have to see a psychiatrist. An MFCC, licensed clinical social worker (LCSW), or psychologist (Ph.D.) will do just fine. Different states call counselors different things. Just be sure that yours is licensed to practice therapy in your state.

First of all, don't call up and say, "Ms. Smith, I think I'm a multiple and do you work with people like me?" Therapists don't take kindly to clients diagnosing themselves. After all, that's what you're paying them big bucks to do. If, on the other hand, you've just moved into a new area, and have already been diagnosed as a multiple, then telling the therapist at the outset is wise.

You say, "Ms. Smith, I'm calling because I'm looking for a therapist. Would you mind answering a few questions for me?" Any therapist worth his or her salt will be willing to give you five minutes on the phone to answer your questions. Some therapists may insist on a first appointment, but won't charge if you don't continue therapy. A person-to-person meeting may help you find out if you can work together.

It's important to remember that most therapists have limited amounts of time between clients. If you're making a phone call, as a matter of simple courtesy, it's a good idea to have your list of questions ready. If you like the answers, make an appointment. If you don't, keep shopping.

When I was shopping, I first went to a woman who had been recommended by my insurance company. She was okay, but we just didn't "click." I wasn't really interested in a male therapist, but Bob's name kept coming up. So, I decided to give him a chance. I made the appointment, and we clicked right away. Keep an open mind. You never know when the right person may appear.

In preparing your list of questions, you need to do a certain amount of soul-searching before you make your first call. As you talk to various therapists, other questions may come to you. Jot them down for the next prospect.

What is really, really, really important to you? Only you can answer this one.

I wanted somebody who made me feel safe, who was concerned with me, who would give me their undivided attention during sessions, and who was trained in hypnosis. Bob fit the bill. I was also impressed when he sent me a questionnaire in the mail asking the basics, so we didn't waste a lot of time on my first visit.

Do you absolutely have to have a therapist that is the same sex as yourself? I have found that working with a male therapist helped me overcome some of my ambivalent feelings toward men. It's been a healthy, growing experience for me to relate to a man in a safe, caring, non-threatening, non-sexual way. Before Bob, I didn't even know it was possible to have a relationship with a man that wasn't a sexual one. You will need to decide for yourself what feels safe and comfortable for you.

If you are gay or lesbian, it's important to let the therapist know during the first phone call. If the therapist is at all homophobic, it will come out then, and you'll have saved yourself the price of admission.

If you would have trouble working with someone with a specific attribute (race, beard, body size, sexual preference, or religious affiliation, for example), it certainly doesn't hurt to ask over the phone. Far better to ask now than waste fifty to a hundred bucks on somebody you won't even consider.

Listed below are some suggested questions. Ask what you're comfortable asking and what pertains to you and your situation.

Here are two basic questions:

1. How much does s/he charge?

2. Does s/he accept insurance?

Then, more specific questions:

3. Does s/he work with adults who were molested as children, or adult children of alcoholics or whatever your history is.

4. How long has s/he been working with survivors?

5. What sort of special training has s/he had? If the therapist has had no specialized training in working with survivors, you may wish to keep shopping for someone a little more knowledgeable.

6. Does s/he think molestation is ever the child's fault? (If you get a therapist who says "Yes," hang up the phone! This one is not for you!)

7. If you know or suspect that you were ritualistically abused, you can ask if the therapist has any experience in this area. If s/he says no, but you've liked everything else so far, find out if s/he is willing to learn.

8. If you speak another language, or are from a different culture, find out if the therapist speaks your language and/or understands that culture. The language barrier is a little hard to get around, and may require you to travel to another area or use an interpreter. Understanding the culture is something that can be learned, if the therapist is willing.

9. How does s/he feel about clients attending support groups or workshops other than those given by the primary therapist? If the therapist feels that s/he is the only source

of healing for you, you may wish to keep shopping if outside workshops and support groups are important to you. Therapists sometimes feel threatened when their clients participate in outside activities. They may fear that they will lose control over the client or that the information the client receives elsewhere will be contrary to their own therapeutic plan. They may simply not want you to become confused by differing points of view, methods, or concepts. They may even be concerned about loss of income. This issue may not come up until after therapy starts. It may be difficult for a therapist to evaluate this question right away.

10. How does s/he feel about contact between sessions? Is the therapist strictly a nine-to-fiver with no contact allowed between sessions? Are extra sessions allowed for crisis? Does the therapist charge for phone calls?

11. If you have a physical disability, is the office wheelchair accessible, or does the building have braille signage for the visually impaired?

After all these questions, and a few of your own that are important to you, you finally decide that Sally Smith, MFCC is the one for you, and you make an appointment.

You arrive at Ms. Smith's office. She's fifteen minutes late starting the session. During your fifty-minute-hour's appointment, she's taken three phone calls from other clients. She excused herself twice to "handle" a colleague's question. She hugged you right away, without your permission, and touches your arm every five minutes. You like her, but feel resentful that you haven't had her all to yourself, and are uncomfortable with all the touching.

My advice? Find another therapist. Whether you click or not, this therapist has some serious boundary and co-dependency issues of her own. You'll save yourself a lot of heartache later if you keep shopping for someone who has time for you, and who respects the privacy of your body.

A good therapist knows that when it's your hour, it's your hour. S/he will forward the phone calls to the receptionist or answering service. S/he listens to you. S/he doesn't touch you without permission.

Let's try another scenario:

You get to the office. Sally Smith comes out, smiles and offers you a cup of coffee. She seems warm and friendly, without being too familiar. Everything is just peachy, you click right away, and feel as if you've known her for years. Wonderful!

But what if she looks just like your great Aunt Matilda who used to beat you with sticks and stuffed foreign objects into your bodily openings? You recoil in horror and think, Good Lord, what do I do now?

Well, you could say, "No, thanks. I've changed my mind," and leave. One confused therapist is a small price to pay for peace of mind.

Or, if possible, you can look at this situation as an opportunity for growth. You accept her invitation into the office, take the coffee, sit down and be honest with her. "Look, this may be really difficult," you say. "You look just like somebody who hurt me a lot when I was a kid, and I'm not sure I can get around that." How she responds will tell you whether you can work together.

What if the longer you're in Sally's office, the more nervous you get? Your guts are in an uproar, you keep wanting to run and hide, you can't look at her face. She looks like Aunt Matilda, talks like Aunt Matilda, and has that same crazy look in her eyes that makes you want to scream and run for cover. Or, you realize this isn't just Aunt Matilda stuff going on here. This lady is weird all on her own.

Nobody says you have to finish the hour, and nobody says you have to go back. If you're that uncomfortable, get out. Listen to your guts. Your instincts have saved your bacon more than once, already. So listen to them, and keep shopping.

Let's try again. The longer you're in Ms. Smith's office, the more comfortable you feel. She forwards the phone to the answering service. She doesn't take a lot of notes, or fidget in her chair. She gives you some personal safety space. She remains warm and friendly. The initial feelings you had over the phone start to come back. This isn't your crazy Aunt Matilda. This isn't the same person that hurt you as a child, but someone entirely different.

If you had run away in the beginning, you might not have known that. You "click."

Congratulations! You've just hired a therapist.

Chapter Six

Self-healing & Therapy

So now you've hired a therapist. Or you've been in therapy for a while and your alters have decided to make themselves known. Where do you go from here?

It's very important for your therapist to get a clear picture of your life outside the therapeutic setting, so be as honest and up-front as you can be.

If you're losing time, you need to tell your therapist. If you woke up this morning and found three new oil paintings drying in the hall, and you don't paint, your therapist needs to know that. If you hear voices in your head, especially if they're telling you to hurt yourself, your therapist needs to know. Your therapist can not help you if s/he doesn't know what's going on.

Lying about your multiplicity may sometimes be a necessary evil, to keep your job, to keep your family, whatever, but lying to your therapist is counterproductive. Painful though it may be, you need to be as open and honest as you can with one person who can really help you.

Memories are kind of like shoes; it's normal to try on somebody else's memory to see if it fits. You may even wear it around for a while, but if it doesn't belong to you, eventually the memory will begin to pinch, and you'll discard it. As you hear other survivors speak, (including me) you may wonder if this or that is a part of your experience, too. You need to trust your own feelings here. If it's your memory, you'll keep it. If it's not, you won't.

Sometimes the memories seem like an endless supply of pain. Just as you work through one experience, another rears its ugly head. It's normal to wonder if this is what the rest of your life is going to be like, just one dreadful memory after another.

The memories of today will have a different quality than the memories of yesterday or the ones of tomorrow. They may even seem to get "worse." What is happening is that your mind is filling in blank spots. A memory you had a month ago may return, with extra details and added insight. A new memory will fill in another piece of the puzzle of your past.

Take heart. Nothing lasts forever, especially not pain. Memories surface as we are able to handle them. After a while, they become fewer and fewer.

I don't know if we ever remember everything. I'm not so sure we need to. As Bob says, "You don't need to count every grain of sand on the beach to know you don't want to build your house there."

Chances are, you see your therapist once or twice a week. But even if you see your therapist more often, or are in a hospital setting, you still need to know how to take care of yourself between sessions.

How do you deal with pain, anger, fear, memories, flashbacks, etc., when you can't have twenty-four-hour-a-day access to your therapist? After all, they go out to dinner, go on vacation and get sick. You need some skills to help you when you're in crisis.

1. If you don't already have a journal, buy one, and start writing.

2. The book *The Courage to Heal*, by Ellen Bass and Laura Davis, features a technique called "stream of consciousness." How it works is: You put your pen to paper and write whatever comes into your head, no matter how silly, foolish or strange it sounds. Keep writing without

stopping until the time you've allotted yourself is up. I like to write for half an hour, which seems to be a manageable length of time for me. It's important to have control over starting and stopping, and still have time to process whatever comes out.

This technique helps bypass those nasty little internal censors. You know, those tiny, insistent voices that are always saying, "Don't tell. I'll kill you if you tell. This is our little secret, so don't tell anybody. It will kill your mother if you tell. Don't tell."

Tell those voices to shut up. It's okay to tell!

Journal writing is one of the most valuable ways to access deeply buried emotions and feelings. It works. Whether you use freewriting, or just sit down and write, it's the most helpful thing I've ever found.

3. If you are not comfortable writing, or even if you are and would like another way to process your pain, I highly recommend getting some art materials. Colored pencils and pens, pastels, water colors, or finger paints can help you get in touch with your feelings.

Or you may wish to color in coloring books, sing, play the radio or a musical instrument, burn incense, or curl up with a teddy bear and cry. All are valuable and helpful ways to express your emotions.

4. Enough, however, is enough. Nobody expects you to deal with your pain all by yourself all the time. You may have been alone when the abuse took place, but you don't have to go through it again by yourself. Reach out. Ask for help. It's okay.

Spend the money and get yourself a phone where all you have to do is push a button and the phone dials the number. Pushing a button is sometimes about all you can handle when you're in crisis. Program the phone numbers of your supportive friends. Make your therapist's number either the first button or the last. It's easier for the children in your system to remember.

Be sure your own phone number and address are clearly displayed on the phone. Your therapist's answering service will ask for your number and your inner kids may not know what it is. Even a singleton's mind goes blank in an emergency, so having your phone number and address prominently displayed could save precious moments when you're in need of help.

Discuss with your therapist who s/he wants you to call first. This is an important issue to resolve in the beginning stages of therapy. Some therapists like to be called first while others prefer you seek assistance from other sources prior to calling them. This is real life, and learning to take care of yourself involves learning to reach out to more than one person.

But, and this is important, engrave it on the inside of your eyelids: It's okay to ask for help. It's okay to call before your crisis reaches epic proportions.

Talk to your friends before a crisis occurs, to see how they feel about midnight phone calls, or calls from your child alters. Your friends provide valuable support, but they have their limits. Develop a network of people to call so you don't burn out one person. They love you, so it's difficult for them to repeatedly hear your pain. Ask them periodically if it's becoming too much for them to handle.

Crisis hotlines are also an excellent resource if you don't feel comfortable calling your friends, especially at 2:00 in the morning!

5. Make a list of things you can do to keep yourself safe when you're in crisis. Tack the list all over the house. Keep a copy in your wallet, in the car and at work. Sometimes just reading the list helps. My list has such things as: Take a deep breath, eat ice cream, hug my teddy bear, call somebody, pet the cat, take a bubble bath, write, and drink some hot

tea. Your list should have as many things on it as are helpful to you.

6. If possible, take a self-defense class. This will not only teach you to defend yourself against further assault, but will raise your self-esteem and confidence. If you choose to do this, it may be helpful to speak with your instructor first. Explain that you are a survivor of childhood trauma, and make sure the class will be appropriate for you. You don't have to disclose your multiplicity if you don't want to.

Some rape crisis centers offer self-defense classes for women, and are empathetic to feelings of survivors. Sometimes, you can get an individual instructor if a class seems too scary.

Let's talk for a minute about therapy itself. Now, far be it for me to tell you and your therapist how to run your therapy. I wouldn't even try. But there are two things that are very important.

One: If your therapist makes a sexual move on you, get out and get out fast. Professional therapy never includes sex in any way, shape, or form. Never! I urge you to report him or her to the authorities immediately. Sadly, there are some therapists who sexually abuse their clients, and they must be stopped.

In all fairness, however, if you suspect your therapist is making a move on you, but you're just not sure, keep your eyes and ears open and your guard up. State your objections clearly and immediately to your therapist. Remember that you're filtering everything through your own abuse. Let your instincts help you. Was it a misunderstanding? If you check it out and your guts tell you you were right, call the appropriate authorities and find a new therapist.

Two: If there is something you want or need from your therapist, ask. Therapists don't run on ESP any more than you do. S/he won't know what you need unless you say so. Be specific. "Next time I'm in a memory like that, would you hold my hand?" "I've written a lot in my journal, and I'd like you to read it." "I've made a collage, and I'd like your opinion." "I need a hug."

Be aware, however, that your therapist may not fulfill your request. Some therapists, as I indicated before, are touchers and some aren't. I have heard some therapists say that they never touch clients. Others go in the opposite direction, using re-parenting techniques and holding the client during their worst memories.

If your therapist does not respond, especially to requests for touch, as you would like, don't take it personally. It's not you! You haven't done anything wrong, and you haven't made an inappropriate request. It simply means that the therapist feels, for whatever reason, that touching may be counterproductive for you at this point.

If you and your therapist have a good working relationship, the issue of touch will be addressed.

As survivors of childhood trauma and multiple personalities, we need to recognize that our whole sense of boundaries is skewed. Sometimes a hug is just a hug. A pat on the back, a squeeze of the arm, or a holding hand are the kind of touches that help us while going through a painful memory. But if you need to be held and comforted while reliving trauma, and your therapist is hesitant, please remember that your therapist is taking a great risk every time s/he touches you in any but the most trivial manner, and may offer some other ideas so you feel comforted and safe.

But what if your therapist insists on touching you, even without your consent? The therapist says, "It's for your own good," or "You need to know that not all touch is bad," or "A little stroke feels good now and then."

My advice? Find another therapist.

Nobody has the right to touch you without your consent. Nobody. Not your therapist, not your boss, not your partner, nobody. Only you decide if it's "for your own good." You have a right to your body, and you have a right to say who touches your body. If you are being touched against your will, whether that touch feels sexual or not, you are being taken advantage of. Get out and shop for another therapist who will respect your wishes.

Besides inappropriate touching, how can you tell if your therapist is behaving in a manner that will ultimately be destructive to you? Here are a few warning signs:

1. Telling sexual jokes or stories.

2. Making comments about your body, or giving you seductive looks. "You look nice, today" can be either an innocent compliment or a come-on. How is it said? Tone of voice? Body language/gestures?

3. Discussing his or her own sex life or problems. Once your therapist starts telling you his or her own problems, therapy stops for you. One warning sign is when you are listening more than you're talking.

4. Becoming friends. Friendship involves mutual sharing, caring and social contact. While you may feel friendly toward your therapist, and your therapist toward you, this feeling is not real friendship. Friendship and therapy are two different things. If your therapy evolves into friendship, find another therapist. The same person can't be both.

5. Asking you out on a date, to lunch, or some other social gathering. This is totally inappropriate!

6. Giving you expensive gifts. Gifts are a bit tricky. I have heard of therapists who regularly remember their client's birthdays with some little trinket, or purchase an inexpensive gift for Christmas. I don't think there is anything inherently wrong with that. Diamond watches or Caribbean Cruises are another matter entirely. Also, beware of gifts with emotional price tags attached. These are gifts that are designed to keep you as a client, or manipulate you into behavior your therapist wants.

7. Suggesting that you do work for the therapist instead of paying the bill. I know, this one seems like the therapist is doing you a favor. The problem is that this creates a tremendous imbalance in the power structure. It's just not a good idea, in addition to being considered unethical (and maybe unlawful) by the profession.

8. Loaning you money or borrowing money from you.

9. Suggesting that you go into business together, no matter what the venture.

10. Renting you office space in his/her building, or living quarters in his/her home.

11. Giving you the impression that you are more "special" than the rest of his or her clients.

12. Demonstrating any behavior that makes you feel uncomfortable, used or abused. You are the most important member of this team. You have the right to the best therapy you can get. Don't let anything stand in the way of getting competent help.

Let's talk for a minute about knowing more about multiplicity than your therapist. If you have multiple personalities, it's likely that you've read every book you can get your hands on. (You're reading this, aren't you?) You've read survivors' stories and you may subscribe to survivors' publications.

If you are your therapist's first multiple client, s/he may be as much in the dark as you are. But wait. First and foremost, is s/he willing to learn? A counselor who is willing to learn is just as good (or maybe better) than somebody with lots of experience.

Learning about multiple personalities for a therapist means reading the clinical literature and survivors' stories, attending workshops and trainings, consulting colleagues and, most importantly, listening to you. After all, you are the one who has multiple personalities. You are the one with first-hand experience and knowledge. It's okay to learn together.

A couple of warnings are in order, however. The diagnosis may change how your therapist works with you, or feels about you. If suddenly you feel like you're under a microscope, or that you've become a "case" rather than a person, or you feel as if your therapist is "experimenting" on you, then it's time to confront the therapist and/or move on. It's impossible to do research and therapy on the same client. It just doesn't work. It's too confusing for both client and therapist.

Therapy, just like any relationship, is bound to have its ups and downs. Sometimes your therapist may do or say something that ticks you off. You feel they don't understand you at all. Here you've spent all morning spilling your guts, and the therapist seems to be off in another world.

Surprise! Therapists are people, too. They have a life outside the office. They come home, eat dinner, make love, and go on vacations. They get the flu and upchuck, just like you do. They have bad days where they wonder if they ever help anybody. They go camping, pay bills, and spend hours in the museum. They argue with their partners and cry at sad movies. They get frustrated with and have fun with their kids. They read books and sing off-key in the shower. They make mistakes.

They have whole days where they don't think about you at all.

Therapists aren't perfect. They're just people.

Chapter Seven

Internal Communication

It's unlikely that you and your alters have perfect communication, especially in the beginning, when you're just getting to know each other. Everyone in the system is scared. The secret is out, and folks will be running for cover.

The early attempts at communication can be confusing and terrifying. This person knows about that person, but that person doesn't know about this one. And this other person just found out about these three over here, and is really upset. And still another just figured out there were others at all! If your head is reeling, then you have a good indication of what it's like to be a multiple. But don't panic. As you learn to communicate with each other, the less chaotic and scary it seems.

In order to get better, good communication is a must. This doesn't happen overnight, by the way. Sometimes this can be a long, slow, frustrating process. Some of your selves will have amnesia for some of the others, so communication can be a difficult task, but not an impossible one.

You may have been hearing the voices of others in your head your whole life, but can't always tell who is speaking. I'll always be grateful to Marta for using a Yorkshire accent, because I can tell when it's she who is speaking. But not everyone in my system is quite so distinctive. And they aren't always willing to share themselves with me.

THE JOURNAL

Using a journal is a vital part of my healing. My alters and I write notes back and forth, and each person gets an opportunity to comment on the day's activities or on what someone else wrote.

After a while, you may be able to tell who is speaking by the handwriting. Not always, however. I have an alter in my system called The Writer, and his job is to write the words, so the handwritings may change even though the same person is speaking, or may stay the same even though different people are speaking. It makes for a very complicated system, and I don't quite understand it. I do know that part of his job is to confuse whoever might be reading the journal, but I don't know why.

For the most part, however, the journal is a valuable tool. Notebooks are inexpensive and readily accessible. Everybody in the system can use it. Even the little ones who can't write can draw pictures in it. And it keeps the information in a central location, which is good for both you and your therapist. Bob gets a copy of just about everything I write. He also has material in his file that I don't have, and don't remember writing.

Another advantage of the journal is that it can monitor progress. I occasionally look back over the journal to see where I was in my healing six months or a year ago, usually when I feel stuck. It helps to see just how far I've come. I'm certainly not in the same place as when I first appeared in Bob's office for therapy, expecting to be "cured" in the first visit! I went through a whole round of uncovering memories, believing it happened, denying it, accepting it finally, and then moving on to the next one.

This journal also tells those folks who reside inside that I care about what they think and how they feel. I may not be able to listen to them all the time, or even know they're there, but with the journal, we can talk to each other.

Another way to use your journal is to just sit at the table and write for a specified length of time each day (called "freewriting," as I mentioned earlier). If it comes into your head, it goes on the paper. Then bring what you wrote to your therapist, no matter how it sounds. What may happen is that not only do your other selves write to you and to each other, they will also write to your therapist.

Some of the people inside are scared. They may want to talk to your therapist, but can't quite bring themselves to do so. Writing in the journal is a way to tell their story, ask questions, or "test the waters" by seeing the therapist's reaction to what was written or drawn.

Another advantage of using the journal to write to your therapist is that it gives everybody a chance to process and work. It tells your therapist who in the system most needs to work this week. Let's face it, it's awfully hard to let thirty-seven people out in the space of a fifty-minute hour, and even if we could, how much work would we get done?

THE TAPE RECORDER

Another method you can use to communicate is the tape recorder. Let your alters tape messages to each other. For alters who cannot read, either because of age or emotional instability, the tapes can be a valuable way to communicate.

The tape recorder can also let you know what happened when you weren't "there." For example, one multiple's husband used to tape the conversations he had with her alters so she wouldn't feel left out when she came "back." In my system, Marta likes to tape stories for the children to play when she's not available.

The tapes can also be valuable for your therapist to hear. Your therapist can't possibly know everything that goes on in your life outside of the therapy session. Taping can be a way to communicate between sessions. Remember that your therapist has limited amounts of time, so check this one out with him or her first! S/he may not take too kindly to twelve sixty-minute tapes appearing on the doorstep each week!

ART

Not everybody writes, and not everybody is comfortable using a tape recorder. Artwork of various kinds can help.

Drawing is a safe way to let out feelings, experiences, wishes, hopes, and fears. Even the children can draw. Drawing can be done in pen, pencil, paint, finger paint or crayon. It can be done on paper, canvas or paper bags, in coloring books or scribble pads.

Use the medium that works best for you, keeping in mind that different alters may use different techniques. The purpose here is processing pain, not creating the next Mona Lisa.

Another form of artwork is the collage. Making a collage involves cutting pictures and words out of magazines or newspapers, and putting them all together on one piece of paper. I like to use 2' x 3' posterboard that you can get at almost any five-and-dime. It's not so much the finished product that is important, but the process itself. This picture goes here, that word goes there, and you don't really understand why until the collage is complete. Sometimes the meaning will jump out at you with startling clarity.

Some survivors create stained glass pictures, embroider, make macrame plant hangers or bake bread. How can these activities help process pain? By allowing each alter a broad range of artistic expression, some of the energy that is used in self-hate and self-blame can be used to create something beautiful and worthwhile. It helps foster a feeling of well-being and self-esteem. It makes us feel better about ourselves.

It's important that everybody in the system has both the opportunity and permission to express themselves.

THE COMMITTEE MEETING

This is a more advanced technique that can be used once you and your alters have gained a high level of communication. In the committee meeting, (sometimes called the board meeting) alters discuss situations, options, and experiences. They also make recommendations and decisions.

As with most committee or board meetings, there is a president, secretary, and treasurer selected by the majority of the internal system. When a decision needs to be made, the committee gets together, thrashes out the options, and comes to a conclusion. The host personality then follows the wishes of the majority (usually).

The committee meeting works for multiples who have reached the level of cooperation or joining (these terms will be explained later). While many multiples feel they have a "committee" going on in their heads all the time, "the committee meeting" differs in that it is a deliberate "getting together" and not a random discussion. Complete agreement may not be reached, but everyone has the opportunity to state their opinions and make their wishes known.

You see, just about every act that you or an alter commits is an attempt to say something. Even the damage caused by a persecutor can be a valuable message. Communication is not limited to words or pictures on a paper.

Chapter Eight

Contracting

A contract is an agreement between two parties to deal with some situation in a mutually acceptable way. For multiples, contracting is an important part of getting along and keeping the system safe.

In my system, for example, the children agree not to come out while we're driving the car, or when I'm at work. Liz agrees not to act on her sexual preference. Millie agrees to let the children into her room when they get scared. And everybody, except The Destroyer, has agreed not to kill themselves.

Contracting can be done with others, as well. You agree not to cut yourself until you call your therapist. You agree to let your significant other or your therapist dole out your medication to you. You agree to call somebody if you get into crisis.

People sometimes get turned off by the word 'contract.' We're not talking about a binding, sign-it-in-blood, reams of paper sort of thing. We're talking about an agreement. Except for the contract regarding suicide, which we'll talk about in a minute, a verbal contract should be just as valid as one on paper.

Contracting is a safety valve for your whole system. The children know they won't wreck the car. Liz knows we won't end up in a divorce because she wanted to dabble in a homosexual relationship. Millie knows that when the kids are safe in her room, they won't be in danger "outside."

Contracting enables you to be free, to go to work and live your life.

Contracts you make with your therapist are usually considered binding by the therapist. That means if your therapist says s/he won't see you any more if you attempt suicide, and you or one of your people cuts your wrists, you are all going to have to live with the consequences.

Contracts need to be made with the entire system in mind. I, for example, have agreed not to send back magazines and catalog items that somebody else has ordered. They, on the other hand, have agreed to keep those items to a minimum. I have agreed to give the children plenty of time to play in the privacy of my own home. For their part, they agree not to come out at social or professional functions.

Sometimes the contract doesn't work. If one of us gets triggered into a flashback or memory, the contract doesn't mean diddley-squat. If that happens, we just deal with it. If one of the little ones comes out in a public place, or if one of the more flamboyant ones decides to make herself known, we just have to reap the consequences later. The truth is that we've been covering up this type of behavior for years, usually without knowing why we've had to do it.

If you are suicidal or are injuring yourself, you may indeed need something in writing. Sometimes the system feels more obligated to follow the contract if it's written down.

A support group for multiples I attended briefly came up with a contract for survival. It works, and it's a tougher contract than any therapist ever thought of. After all, we know where the loopholes are, don't we?

CONTRACT FOR SURVIVAL

To cover the period of ________________ to ______________

I/We ______________________________________ ________________ agree not to knowingly or intentionally cause serious or fatal bodily harm or injury, including those actions which could result therein (i.e. overdose, reckless driving, etc.) to this physical, mental, emotional or spiritual body.

I/We will not knowingly kill, physically, mentally, emotionally or spiritually, ourselves or any other person or personality.

As protectors, we the undersigned, to the best of our ability, agree to intervene on behalf of our other persons or personalities who may be unable or unwilling to do so, by calling and actually reaching and connecting with the support members listed on this form.

When I call a support person, I will state that I am ca ling because of the contract and we will honestly address and discuss the emotions and events that led to crisis and the possible solutions and safety measures to be taken. We will continue to pursue all phone numbers, including repetitions, until the crisis is resolved.

In the event of breaking or attempting to break this contract, professional intervention may be contacted and requested.

Anyone who has reservations about signing this contract must voice them now or you are bound by this contract for the duration of the contract period.

This contract is valid past the end date until a new contract has been negotiated or all support members of the previously agreed upon contract have been contacted and agree that relinquishment of this contract is in the best interests of the contractee.

____

Signature of Host Personality

____

Signatures of those who agree to intervene on behalf of the host and others in the system:

____

____

____

____

____

____

I object to the signing of this contract. I will discuss my reasons here:

____

____

____

____

These are the persons/agencies I agree to call:

Name and Phone Number

____

____

____

____

____

____

I, the undersigned support person(s) agree to provide emotional or physical support to the contractee within the terms of this contract. I understand the contractee may contact me any time of the day or night.

____

____

____

____

Now, that's a binding contract! The group spent hours on it, and I think it's a good one. Show it to your therapist and see what s/he thinks about it. Feel free to copy it and use it word for word. (I know this book is copyrighted, but this is an exception.)

Just remember that contracting is only as good as you all make it. The better you communicate, the better you can contract, and the better your life will be.

Chapter Nine

Covering Up Versus Coming Out

The thought of revealing your multiplicity can be frightening, even for those who have come to terms with the diagnosis. Because of the public's misconceptions about this condition, a revelation of multiplicity may cause serious repercussions in your personal life

Your life may be chaotic, or it may be fairly calm and stable, or cycles of both. Every person's life and circumstances are different and you have the right to choose whether or not to disclose at all, and if so, to whom and how much.

Disclosure carries both risks and benefits, but before we discuss these, we need to look at the basics of telling. The important thing to remember is that you have many choices and things to consider:

1. Why tell

2. Who to tell

3. When to tell

4. How to tell

5. How much to tell

WHY TELL?

Why tell? Of all the questions, this is perhaps the most difficult to answer. You need to ask yourself what you hope to accomplish by telling people you have multiple personalities.

Are you telling your abusers so you can say, "See, this is what you did to me?"

Are you telling your friends so they will feel sorry for you?

Are you telling because it makes you feel special and different?

Are you telling to get attention?

Are you telling so you can write about it later?

Ouch. That hurt. I said those things because those are exactly the kinds of things I said to myself as I was telling people about my multiplicity. I was terribly afraid that I was disclosing for my own selfish interests, that I wasn't really a multiple at all, and I was just saying it to get attention. All the negative things that could go through a person's head went through mine.

And the answer, for me, was "no." When I really looked at why I was telling, I was really saying, "child abuse is wrong! This is what child abuse did to me. I didn't do anything wrong, and I'm a strong, courageous person who survived."

I wanted people to know that multiples are not people to fear. I wanted people who knew me to know that I was still me, and knowing about my multiplicity didn't make me different. I wanted them to understand why I sometimes acted in ways that were out of character, so they wouldn't be offended if one of my more outrageous alters came out.

I wanted my inside people to know that I was not ashamed to acknowledge them publicly. After all, they're the reason I'm alive today, talking and telling. Talking and telling. They saved my life and they saved my sanity. Why on earth should I be ashamed of them?!

Before you tell, ask yourself why you are telling. Why are you telling this particular person? What do you hope to gain or accomplish? Don't tell until you have an answer that satisfies you.

WHO TO TELL

Consider starting with your partner. If you are in a significant relationship with someone, married or not, that person needs to know what's going on with you. If you have a therapist, schedule a joint session, and have the therapist explain your condition to your partner and how it manifests itself in your particular case. Your partner may have a tough time dealing with this, and you need to know if s/he can handle it. If you don't have a therapist, you may want to have your partner read something before you talk to him/her directly.

Next, you may want to tell your best friend. See how that person responds. As your feelings of comfort and safety grow, continue to tell friends that you think will be the most supportive. You may be asking some of these people for help in a crisis and you need to know if they'll be there for you.

You may or may not wish to tell your family. If your family are the ones who caused your trauma in the first place, they may not be supportive. On the other hand, family members who were not directly involved in the abuse may be some of your best sources for support and validation. Disclosing your multiplicity may be a vital part of confrontation with your abusers. I refer you to the chapter on confrontation in the book *The Courage To Heal*, which covers the topic thoroughly.

You may or may not wish to tell your boss and/or your co-workers, for reasons we'll talk about later.

Who you tell is up to you. Let your instincts be your guide.

WHEN TO TELL

Ideally, telling people about your multiplicity should only be done when you are comfortable with the diagnosis. After you and your therapist have reached an understanding about who you all are, then a discussion about disclosure is in order.

If possible, pick your time and place carefully. Make it on your turf, in surroundings you are comfortable with, and have a support person nearby if that seems appropriate.

You may want to tell via a letter rather than in person. Sending a letter saves you from having to respond to the person's belief or disbelief immediately. It gives you the opportunity to say what you really want to say without being interrupted, walked out on, attacked, vilified or abused. It gives you time and space to choose your words carefully.

Sometimes, though, circumstances may dictate disclosure because someone sees you switch, and the personality who comes out is so unlike you that you have to tell. In a situation like this, it helps if you can at least get the person to a private location. This can be heavy news to hear, as well as tell.

HOW TO TELL

How you tell is fairly easy. It's possible the person you are telling has noticed that you sometimes act in confusing ways. They think you are moody, or childish, or suspect something is wrong, and just don't know what. So telling simply involves putting a label on it. Conversely, others may be completely surprised. They may never have knowingly met more than one or two of your personalities.

You may have to lead up to it gently. After all, people react in a variety of ways to such news. Don't take their first response at face value. A "no way!" response doesn't necessarily mean this person is going to be unsupportive. We all deal with denial in different ways. Give the person a chance.

So, what do you say? Something like: "I need to tell you something about me. This is really hard for me, because I don't know how you're going to respond, but you're an important person in my life and I'd like you to know this about me."

"I have a condition called multiple personalities. You may have seen the movie *Sybil*, or *The Three Faces of Eve*. Well, what I have is kind of like that." Then go on to explain how your condition manifests itself. If the person has already met some of your alters, you can share that. Now is probably not the time for introductions, but that can certainly be done at a later date.

Before you disclose your multiplicity to anyone, it's helpful to practice your disclosure and possible reactions with your therapist. Be prepared for unexpected reactions. It's common to program yourself for someone's disbelief, anger, or fear, and not be prepared if the person acts supportively. Or, if you anticipate support and get the opposite, you may be devastated and hurt.

Covering up versus coming out. Your life. Your choice.

Always, your choice.

HOW MUCH TO TELL

How much to tell is a matter of individual preference. Your therapist needs to know everything. But a business associate may need to know nothing.

If your significant other is a valuable part of your support system, s/he may need to know how to help you, but may not need to know the "gory details" of your abuse. I'm not so sure the details are necessary, and in fact, they could be detrimental to your relationship. On the other hand, certain activities and actions may trigger flashbacks of abuse, and without explaining some details, your partner may become confused and frightened.

The same goes for your friends and family. You may even wish to share more of the details with certain friends than with your partner. Support groups are often good places to discuss details and receive comfort and validation not usually found elsewhere. Generally, other survivors can handle the details better than anyone else. However, sometimes members of support groups may try to outdo each other with their tales of abuse. This "contest" can ultimately destroy the group. It's important for everyone in the group to know that they belong. No one can judge the impact of the abuse on your life except you – and on their lives except them.

Sharing details with supportive family members may help both you and the other person validate each other's experiences. Disclosing details prematurely, however, could destroy your relationship with that person, especially if they have never dealt with their own abuse or if their horror is too overwhelming.

How much you discuss is up to you. It's important not to be bullied into sharing more than you are willing to risk.

RISKS OF TELLING

Every time you tell somebody about your multiplicity, you are taking a risk. You risk losing the support of a family member, a friendship or a job.

Telling your boss and/or co-workers can be risky. If you or your alters are acting out at work, and your boss is looking for an excuse to fire you, this could be it. Legally, you cannot be fired simply because you're a multiple. You can only be terminated for actual performance problems.

In the beginning, I was terribly afraid to tell my boss, for fear she would think I was too dangerous to work with clients and I would lose my job. But the pressure of not telling became greater than the fear, and I finally told her. She was wonderful! (She also wasn't particularly surprised.) She even went to the board of directors and explained my condition to them. I found such wonderful support from everybody that my healing took a dramatic turn for the better. Be aware, however, that not everybody's boss is as understanding as mine.

If you are in a position of authority or prestige in your community, you may want to keep your multiplicity between you and your therapist. Society is still fearful of what they don't understand.

Don't be surprised if people try to talk you out of your diagnosis. They may give you excuses as to why you can't possibly be a multiple. They may cite their misconception that multiplicity is rare and, therefore, you couldn't have it. They may tell you they've never seen any evidence of your multiplicity. They may believe there is no such thing.

It's likely that your family of origin has been keeping the secret of abuse for many years and may feel threatened and afraid. Family members who once seemed supportive may no longer want contact with you. Your abusers may accuse you of lying and try to make you doubt your own reality. You may be told that you're making it up, or that you're just saying this to get attention or to hurt the family. It's also possible they may reject your disclosure because accepting it means admitting that the abuse happened.

Your partner and children may become frightened and distant. They could be just as fearful as society at large and will need assurances that you are the same person you have always been. It's important to include them in your therapy as much as possible, if that's helpful. They're going to be confused, afraid, and upset, but there's a part of them that's also going to be relieved. Your unpredictable behavior now has an explanation.

If your partner is not supportive, or you are caught in the web of an abusive relationship, your healing may suffer. Sometimes partners would prefer that you stay the way you are, as you may be easier to control. It's terribly easy to manipulate a multiple, and an abuser may have a vested interest in making you think you're crazy.

If you are in an abusive relationship, work with your therapist to help you gain the self-esteem you need to extricate yourself.

Your children may learn to call out specific alters for their own purposes. They may want to play with some of your inner children or you may have an alter who is a more lenient parent than you. Your children need to know that manipulating you may be counter-productive for everyone in the long run.

Your partner may find it exciting to have sexual relations with different alters. This manipulation only increases the division between the selves and should be discouraged.

Invitations from friends to bowling or dinner may become few and far between. People don't want to look you in the eye, or they may watch you for signs of switching. They become overly concerned about "who you are now." You will definitely find out who your real friends are.

BENEFITS OF TELLING

The positive side is that every time you tell somebody about your multiple personalities, you are also telling the perpetrators that you will no longer be silent. You are telling the world that child abuse is wrong, and that you are doing everything in your power to stop it. You are being open and honest about who you are.

You may find new friends and discover that old ones had also been abused. Your courage in disclosing your multiplicity may inspire others to seek help for their own child abuse issues. You may find that some people you know are also multiples.

Just as telling your boss and co-workers can be risky, it can also be positive. If you're doing a fine job, and you aren't missing a lot of work because of your multiple personalities, then you're going to be an example of how this doesn't have to be a debilitating condition. Not to mention, they may be getting the talents of several people in one neat little package – you!

You may feel a sense of relief that you don't have to hide this part of your life any more. So much of your energy has been spent keeping secrets. Telling about your abuse and about your condition is ripping the lid off the secret and exposing child abuse for the horror it really is.

I'm not saying you have to wear a shirt reading "I Have Multiple Personalities," but I am saying that being a multiple is nothing to be ashamed of. It helps people understand you, who you really are and where you came from. It helps others become honest with themselves and with you. It inspires other multiples and child abuse survivors to share their own pain. The more knowledge and education the public receives about multiple personalities, the less frightened it will be. And who is more qualified to teach them?

The choice is yours. As I said, you may choose to tell some people and not others. You may still not want to tell anybody. If you are going around the Maypole of denial, it may be difficult to tell when even you're not sure. Not everybody needs to come out in print with their multiplicity. I have simply chosen to make mine public as an aide to my own healing, and hopefully, to help you along the road with yours.

Chapter 10

Work

Work is probably one of the best ways that I keep my sanity and stability. Working raises my self-esteem and helps me give something back to those who helped me. Not to mention putting cereal on the table in the morning.

Now, I understand that some of you can't work. Sometimes the internal pressure is too much. If you are switching too much to hold down a job, then working may not be an option at this time.

You may be switching so much that you can't possibly maintain a job. Your alters come out at work and yell at customers. Your kids come out and screw up the computer. You have so much amnesia for your activities that you show up for work one morning only to find you haven't been there in three months.

If this is where you are, then don't beat yourself up for not working. If you can't, you can't, and that's okay. As you work on your issues in therapy, you will get stronger. Your alters will learn to cooperate, join or integrate. Your life will become more stable, and working may become an option that isn't available to you now.

Maybe a paying job that expects you at regular hours every day is not for you, but there are other options. You can volunteer on an irregular, on-call basis for your favorite charity or organization. Women's shelters, the March of Dimes, or the American Cancer Society all love volunteers.

The sense of self-worth and value that you feel, just by spending a little time like this, is well worth it.

But there is a big difference between "can't work," and "won't work." If you can work, you should work. I'm not being hard-nosed about this. One of the ways abusers continue to "win" is by making us think we're helpless. But we're not helpless! We've made it this far, haven't we?

A big part of "working on yourself" is learning to live in the real world. In the real world, people go to work and make money to take care of themselves and their families. Yes, you were hurt terribly as a child. You have a condition that makes working difficult. You need to work on your issues. But the world does not owe you a living. You owe it to yourself to try to be as independent as possible.

I believe we remain prisoners of our past only as long as we choose to. In the beginning, I would have been outraged to hear that. I wasn't choosing pain! God knows I would rather have spent my life doing something (anything!) other than curling up on my living room floor, howling with the pain of yet another memory. And yet, as I look back on it, I see that I did have a choice, and my choice was to be in pain. Somehow, I knew that the only way to not be in pain, was to let the pain happen. And I chose to remain in that prison until I felt safe enough to come out.

We remain prisoners by becoming alcoholics, drug addicts, compulsive overeaters and gamblers. We run from relationship to relationship, hoping "this time" will be different. We stuff our memories with cigarettes and coffee. Or we become overachievers, successful business people who always feel like imposters or workaholics.

The only way to escape is to stop. Stop drinking, stop smoking, stop taking drugs, stop overeating, stop gambling. Stop running away from your memories and your past. You need to feel everything, remember as much as you can, and do something worthwhile every day. And sometimes that "something" can be just getting up and going to work.

Work can be a lifesaver. It gives us a handle on the real world and keeps us grounded and stable. Work raises our self-esteem, puts cookies in the lunch bucket, and sometimes provides the insurance coverage that helps us work with a good therapist.

Work can make us feel free.

It can be scary. I know. But you can do it! You didn't get to be 20, 30, 40, 50 years old by being stupid, weak or helpless. You are a strong, courageous person, or you would have died long ago. You've got more guts than you give yourself credit for. Go ahead and give it a try.

What if you try and you fall on your face? At least you tried. And there will be other opportunities later. I don't believe in failure. I think failures are simply opportunities whose time wasn't quite right. If you tried, even if it didn't work, then you didn't fail. The only failure is never to try.

Let's look at the other side of the coin. You've been working your whole life. Your multiplicity is on the mild end of the scale. You work a nine-to-five and haven't missed a day of work in twelve years. Your alters may come out at home or in therapy, but rarely at work, and if they do, people just think you're moody.

Or, maybe you hold a responsible position in the community. You're a doctor, lawyer, counselor, or policeman. You spend half your life in fear that the "secret" of your multiplicity will come out and ruin your career.

This is important, so let's look at some survival skills for the workplace.

Remember contracting? This is one of the places where you must contract. Get together with your alters and decide who works.

For example, there are three of us who do my job: myself, Roberta and Kate. I'm "there" most of the time, but Kate likes to talk to the domestic violence victims and do the public speaking. Roberta is an excellent counselor, and works especially well with adults who were molested as children, as well as rape victims.

At one point, Regina was coming out at work, and we had to contract to keep her inside. She's only thirteen and doesn't understand about keeping your cool at work. She'll still sneak out occassionally and have a cigarette. And once, my co-worker Mary was reciting a children's poem, and she almost had a three-year-old in her lap, so we had to contract with Mary not to do that anymore!

I know this is going to sound like I'm caretaking, but one of the best survival skills for the workplace is to take care of yourself. Eat healthy meals. Get plenty of rest and exercise. Read something other than survivors' stories for a while. Take care of yourself. Your alters are more likely to act out if you're not taking care of the physical body you all share. And what better place to give yourself attention than at work?

The whole trick to working is to let your alters have internal input as much as possible, without overtly switching. It can be done, and if everybody understands the benefits, then the system is more likely to cooperate with you.

If your boss or co-workers know about your multiplicity, it can reduce a lot of the tension and strain. If one of your alters gets too outrageous, your co-workers can ask for "you" back. Or they can get a different viewpoint on some particular problem. The old saying is that two heads are better than one. In our case. . . boy, is the boss getting a bargain!

Chapter Eleven

Goals

Back in the olden days (a couple of years ago), it was thought that the only "cure" for multiple personalities was totally integrating all parts of the self. That view is now changing. There are several choices to consider: remaining a multiple, cooperation, joining, and integration.

It's important to remember that your goals are the ones that matter. Your therapist may be working towards integration, but your internal system may reject that as an option. What you want is what counts. Just be aware that what you want or decide may change with time.

REMAINING A MULTIPLE

Yes, remaining a multiple is an option. However, clinical literature suggests that multiples who choose to retain their multiplicity also retain a certain amount of unresolved trauma. Dr. Frank Putnam, in his book *Diagnosis and Treatment of Multiple Personality Disorder*, says that multiples choose to remain multiples for a variety of reasons.

Sometimes a multiple will leave therapy because trauma s/he is uncovering is just too painful. Leaving therapy allows the person to bury the trauma yet again, for a while anyway, and leaves the defense of multiplicity in place. Other people choose to remain multiples because they see the loss of alters as a death, and alters themselves fear "dying." Nobody can see the advantages of being just one person when this defense has worked for years. Alters want to remain themselves. Multiples are often afraid that if they get "well," their therapist will no longer be interested in them. They are afraid that being a singleton will disrupt the relationships in their lives. They also fear the loss of their main defense mechanism, and are concerned they won't be able to handle stress and crisis without it. And some multiples just plain like to be multiples. There is a certain amount of secondary gain to be had by claiming the label, much as we hate to admit it. You are a bit of an authority on the subject, certainly where your friends are concerned. If you are a writer or a public speaker, then the public is slightly more interested in an active multiple than an integrated one.

COOPERATION

Many multiples opt for cooperation, especially when they are working toward integration. Cooperation among a multiple's system is exactly the same as cooperation between singletons.

With cooperation, everybody knows everybody else. Alters watch out for each other, and everyone works together for the good of the entire system. It's like holding hands on a large scale.

One of the advantages of cooperation is that everybody gets to remain themselves. Nobody "dies." Everybody has a say in the everyday activities of life. Everybody gets to have a life of their own, within the structure of the group.

A disadvantage of cooperation versus integration is that the challenges of multiplicity still exist. Just as any large group of singletons can't always agree on everything, all of your alters are not likely to agree all the time either. This can cause dissention within the system, and a further splitting of the group. It can also cause acting out among alters who aren't getting their own way. Cooperation works well when it works. When it doesn't, it can be a disaster.

JOINING

The concept of joining is not one you will find in clinical literature. This concept was created in my system and may work for yours.

Joining is a midway point between cooperation and integration. Joining can be compared to a fruitcake. Once the fruitcake is baked, the green cherries remain green cherries and the pecans stay pecans. Yet the cake, with all its varied parts, is considered one whole thing.

In joining, the alters get to remain themselves, yet can join forces to complete tasks or handle situations. Usually the host personality is designated to live in the world, with internal input from the rest of the system. They work cooperatively to see that the system functions well, yet are available with their individual talents to handle crises or danger.

Personally, I like the concept of joining very much. Many of my people fought the idea of integration, seeing integration as death. However, they and I cooperate on a grand scale. You may remember I was talking about how I function at work. Kate, Roberta and I "join" at work to get the job done. Even when Roberta is counselling, Kate and I are as much a part of her as if we were her. When Kate is speaking in public, she gets lots of input from Roberta and I, yet we are as much on stage as she is. We are joined, which is a step beyond cooperation, but isn't quite integration. I realize joining and cooperation appear to be very similar. In cooperation, the selves are making separate decisions within the system, but joining actually creates a temporary merger of the selves.

I know that sounds a little complicated, but it's a system that seems to be working for us. If this sounds like a happy alternative for your system, talk it over with your therapist and see what s/he says. Remember, just because something is working for me at this point in my life doesn't mean it's going to work forever, or that it will work for you. You and your therapist are the experts here, not me.

INTEGRATION

Many therapists still view integration as the ultimate goal of therapy. For some multiples, it is the most logical and desirable result.

Integration is like a chocolate cake. You take the flour, the milk, the egg and the chocolate, mix it all together, bake it, and it comes out one whole thing. You're never going to get the egg back as only an egg, or the milk as milk.

Integration means that all parts of yourself that are currently split off meld into one single personality. Therapists will tell you that nobody dies, per se, but it is true that the personalities no longer exist as separate individuals.

Talents and interests of your alters will, after the dust settles, become a part of your own make-up. You should feel stronger and more solid.

Sometimes your alters may integrate on their own, with no assistance from you or your therapist. This spontaneous integration usually occurs when fragments have remembered and shared their trauma with the rest of the system. Occasionally, alters who serve similar functions may integrate on their own.

It is important to remember, though, that integration is only one option. The choice of which option to pursue is up to you. You need to discuss all of them with your therapist and keep in mind that your decision about goals may change over time. Just keep an open mind.

Chapter Twelve

Recovery Means Moving On

Whether you choose to remain a multiple, seek cooperation, joining or integration, there are some issues that need to be dealt with throughout your journey.

GRIEF

Grieving is a natural part of recovery. It's normal to grieve for your lost innocence, your lost childhood and the part of your life that "might have been" if you had not been abused. Grieving hurts, but it also heals, and I don't think you can truly recover without it.

Tears are nature's way of telling us we hurt. Even though we may be crying because we are angry, underneath is still grief. So much was taken from you – things that every child ought to have. Your innocence, safety and ability to trust and have loving relationships were all damaged by abuse. You have every right to grieve for those things.

If integration is one of your goals, you will also find yourself grieving the "loss" of your alters. Sometimes, especially when integration happens spontaneously, you may feel cheated that you didn't have more time to get to know the people who saved your life. It seems just as you get to know them, like them, and begin to appreciate all they did for you, they leave. Naturally, this can bring up old feelings of abandonment, only this time from within.

It feels lonely inside. You don't hear the voices so much, or maybe not at all. Your life has mellowed out to something vaguely akin to boredom. You miss your inside people. There seems to be an empty place where chaos and your alters used to live.

But they are not really gone.

Just as a drop of rain loses its identity when it falls into a river, it goes on to live as part of the river. So it is with you. Your alters may lose their "separateness" to integration, but will always remain a part of you. After all, they were never really anything else.

It's okay to grieve for them, for their separateness, for their uniqueness, for the loss of defense they represent. They were a separate part of you for a lot of years, and it's going to feel empty and sad. Just remember that they're still with you, just in a different form. Remember the chocolate cake? You're now one whole thing, not just the sum of your parts.

Recovery means grieving, and grieving means letting go. Letting go of what might have been. Letting go of what should have been. Letting go of shame. Letting go of fear. Letting go of the fantasy life you had built for yourself. Letting go of your alters. And anytime we have to let go of anything, we grieve.

It's okay. You have a right to your sadness.

It helps to know that as you let go of the strings that tie you to your past and relieve yourself of the burdens of your memories, you will be more free to meet your future.

SEX

Whether you are heterosexual, homosexual, bisexual or celibate, sex is an issue that ultimately must be addressed. For some multiples, it's the last part of therapy. For others, it's ongoing throughout. And for yet others, it's an issue that never completely gets resolved.

As you begin to become sexually active again, if you've been celibate for a while, it's going to feel frightening. Many of the old issues of trust, abandonment, revictimization, guilt and shame may resurface. It's important for you and your partner to work together with your therapist to resolve these feelings.

If you've been sexually active all along, these very same issues may trouble your relationship. It may be helpful to involve your partner in the therapeutic process.

The whole topic of sex is covered very well in *The Courage To Heal*, and a book by Wendy Maltz, *Sexual Healing Journey*, so I won't dwell on it much here. Your sexual self is one part of you that your abusers may have damaged, but I don't believe any of us, or any part of us is damaged beyond repair. As you heal in other areas of your life, this part can heal as well. A good therapist and an understanding partner can do wonders for you. Be open to new opportunities, and allow yourself to feel the joy that sex can bring to a relationship.

DENIAL

One of the most difficult aspects of recovering from child sexual abuse in general, and multiplicity in particular, is denial. We're all familiar with The Voice of Denial. This is the voice inside our head who says, "You're making all this up, you know," and "None of this ever really happened," and "You're just doing this for attention," and "How can you say this? Your parents (brother, aunt, teacher, etc.) really loved you. They would never hurt you."

I think denial has gotten a bad rap. In some cases, I'm not so sure that denial is a bad thing. It's a built-in defense mechanism that prevents us from getting too much, too fast. Denial provides us with a resting place where we can take a breather from memories and pain. Without it, we'd be overwhelmed with the enormity of our abuse. If we were inundated with wave after wave of memories and truths, and we had to accept each one with no respite, it might be too much for us.

Denial helps us heal at a pace that is safe for us.

Acceptance of your multiple personalities has the defense of denial built right in. You can accept your diagnosis one minute and totally reject it the next. It's part of the package.

Believing you're a multiple means believing that you really were abused, that you didn't live in Beaver Cleaver's house, and that somebody you may have loved and trusted hurt you. That's hard. So denial comes in and says "Me? Abused? Of course not!" Denial gives us hope that maybe somehow we made a mistake. Maybe none of it is true.

But denial is only the reverse of the coin. The other side is acceptance. Yes, it is true. Yes, you were hurt. Yes, you do have multiple personalities. Just be aware that flipping the coin is part of the process.

AN END AND A BEGINNING

I hope this book has been helpful to you. Healing from the effects of child abuse and learning to live with multiple personalities can be a long and painful process, as well as an exciting and liberating one. I hope this book was able to make your journey a little easier and that you will reread the sections you found most helpful. Different sections can be useful at different stages of your recovery.

Please, show this book to your therapist, if s/he hasn't already read it. Get their opinion. Your therapist knows you and the circumstances of your life. I don't. I can only hope that some of what helped me, will help you, too.

Good luck, and peace. . . to all of you.

Terminology

Throughout this book, I have used a number of different terms. Most of them you may be familiar with, but some may be new to you, especially if you are just beginning the recovery process.

MULTIPLE PERSONALITY DISORDER is the official term for the condition of having two or more separate persons or personalities who inhabit the same body, and at least two of these persons or personalities take control of the person's behavior. This is also known as MPD, multiple personality defense, multiplicity or just multiple personalities.

The PERSONS OR PERSONALITIES who reside inside are called by a variety of different names: alternate personalities, alters, parts, the others, my friends, my inside kids, my people, the host personality, the original child. As you talk to other multiples, you may hear other terms. You may use other terms yourself. I sometimes talk about "my system," or "the company."

Your ALTERS may be male or female, children, adolescents or adults, protectors or persecutors. They are explained more fully in the text. Your HOST PERSONALITY is generally the one who spends most of the time living in the world. This is the one who carries the legal name, writes the checks to the therapist, and has the most percentage of "body time."

A FRAGMENT is a personality who only carries a memory or two, or who has a very limited function. This fragment is not as fleshed out as a true alter, and usually has very little body time.

SINGLETONS are people with one personality, also called "normies" or just plain folks – not always healthy folks, but folks who don't have multiple personalities just the same.

The VOICES are the different voices you hear in your head when your alters talk to you or speak amongst themselves. Sometimes this can be frightening, especially if you don't understand what's going on. But for some of us, we've heard the voices for so long, we consider it normal.

To SPLIT is to create a new personality, usually in response to fresh trauma. Clinical literature suggests that in order for multiple personalities to occur, the first split needs to have occurred before the age of five. However, once the defense of splitting is in place, new alters may be created up into adulthood. Splitting occasionally happens in therapy, as trauma is uncovered.

To SWITCH is to move from one personality state into another. Sometimes this is in response to perceived danger from the outside, or from inside memories. Alters will switch in therapy, as different people come out to work on their own issues. Sometimes, alters will come out for only a few minutes or a few seconds and then go back in. When many alters do this in the space of a short time, I call it 'the revolving door.' This can be very frightening for the multiple, and for the alters as well, especially if nobody knows what's going on.

DISSOCIATION is a defense mechanism in which a person's mental processes are segregated in order to avoid emotional distress, or where an idea or object is separated from its emotional significance. There are many levels of dissociation, from "highway hypnosis" or bored inattention that is common to most people, to multiple personalities.

In one of the chapters, I talk about feeling STUCK. Feeling stuck is when you look at your therapy, and you look at your life, and nothing seems to be happening. You don't think you're getting better. You aren't having any new memories to work on. You feel like you're in limbo, waiting for something to happen. That's frustrating, but okay. Just think of these periods as a breather, and enjoy them while you've got them.

CO-DEPENDENCY is when you put another person's needs and wishes before your own most of the time.

RITUAL ABUSE can mean many things. It can mean that you were abused at the hands of a satanic or satanic-like cult or coven. It can mean that you were abused in a ritualistic manner, which can be anything from a home-grown cult to every time Uncle Charley gave you hot chocolate before you went to bed meant he was going to come in and abuse you that night.

Ritual abuse survivors have recalled being sexually abused by men, women and other children. Murder, cannibalism, and bestiality are common themes for survivors.

It's important to remember that not all multiples were ritually abused, and not all people who were ritually abused become multiples.

One of the most difficult terms to define is BOUNDARIES. A boundary is not a fence and it's not a wall. It doesn't mean that you never let anyone inside, but that you don't let other people take advantage of you. As children, abusers violated our bodies and therefore violated our boundaries. When we've never had any, it's difficult to learn them as adults.

Boundaries may make us angry. We want our therapist all to ourselves, and we get angry when s/he has another client to attend to.

Boundaries may make us sad. We want our friends to hold us and comfort us, and they may be too overwhelmed or busy to do so.

And boundaries make us feel strong. The next-door neighbor wants us to baby-sit. . . again, and we say "no," without feeling guilty.

Healthy boundaries means acting in a self-assertive manner. It means knowing where you start and the outside world stops.

Things To Do And Things To Read

There are a number of excellent books and publications on the market, many that discuss multiplicity in some detail. There are also some good workshops and support groups to attend. I'll list a few of my favorites here, with my reasons. I try to give prices whenever possible, but keep in mind that prices change.

As always, check with your therapist regarding workshops and support groups. Some can be quite stressful and may be counter-productive.

BOOKS

The Courage To Heal, by Ellen Bass and Laura Davis is published by Harper & Row, New York. You can get it at almost any bookstore and it costs about $18.00. It will be the best money you can spend, outside of good therapy. In addition to excellent chapters on confronting your abusers, sex, and remembering, it was the one book that helped me feel that I wasn't crazy. It told me the abuse wasn't my fault. It gave me tools to help my healing. It's wonderful!

Ellen Bass and Louise Thornton co-edited a book called *I Never Told Anyone, Writings By Women Survivors Of Child Sexual Abuse*. Like *The Courage To Heal*, I found a great deal I could identify with, and it helped me to feel less alone. Good book. Harper & Row, New York.

Sybil by Flora Schreiber is a classic in the field. It's graphic and stunning, but full of hope for the survivor. This one is out in paperback, so should only cost $6.00 - $8.00.

You can also probably find this one in the library or in second-hand book stores.

When Rabbit Howls by The Troops for Truddi Chase is an outstanding book. I could relate completely to the confusion that multiplicity can cause. Truddi gave me hope that multiplicity didn't have to be debilitating, and that I/we could live normal lives. Published by E. P. Dutton, New York. $18.95 hardcover.

Eliana Gil, Ph.D. wrote a little book in 1984 called *Outgrowing the Pain* published by Launch Press ($5.95 soft cover). This is a book for individuals who fear they may have been abused as children. It is a gentle introduction to the topic of child abuse in general and helps readers to understand the general consequences of being abused as a child. Dr. Gil has written a new book, *Outgrowing the Pain Together: A Book for Spouses and Partners of Adults Abused as Children* (Dell, July 1992), which provides education and guidance for those individuals in relationships with adult survivors. She also has a book out on multiplicity called *United We Stand.* When I first saw the book, which is written in a very simple format, I thought, "Oh, Dear!" I was really afraid it was going to talk down to us. I was pleasantly surprised. The book presented information about multiple personalities in a form that all the members of my system could understand, without being too simple. I appreciated that, and so did the rest of the company. I've met her briefly at a couple of professional functions, and she's just as nice in person as her many books imply. Published by Launch Press. $5.95 soft cover.

Give Me Wings! An Incest Survivor's Journal Of Recovery, by yours truly. (You know I had to get my book in here somewhere!) During my recovery, I published a book of poetry and prose that dealt with many aspects of my healing, including my multiplicity. This book costs $7.00 and is available from:

Morning Star, Ltd.
P O Box 5305
Cottonwood, CA 96022

Suffer The Child by Judith Spencer is only for the stout-hearted. This is a graphic and riveting tale of satanic ritual abuse, and should be read with caution. It was valuable for me, but check with your therapist first, and read this one with a support person available. Published by Pocket Books, a division of Simon & Schuster, New York. $4.95 soft cover.

Other books I've found interesting and helpful have been:

Katherine, It's Time by Kit Castle and Stefan Bechtel

Voices by Trula LaCalle

The Minds Of Billy Milligan by Daniel Keyes

My Father's House by Sylvia Fraser

Ghost Girl by Torey Hayden

Diagnosis And Treatment Of Multiple Personality Disorder by Dr. Frank Putnam

MPD From The Inside Out published by Sidran Press

Multiple Personality Disorder (MPD) Explained For Kids published by University of North Carolina, Chapel Hill, NC

The Flock by Joan Frances Casey and published by Alfred A. Knopf

NEWSLETTERS

Many Voices is probably my favorite newsletter. If I had to let all the others go, I'd keep this one. Many Voices is written specifically for multiples. In addition to the traditional survivors' pieces, this newsletter often has articles by therapists.

The artwork is outstanding. Lynn, one of the regular contributors of art to many of the survivors' magazines, is particularly excellent.

The cost at this time is $30.00 per year. Contact:
Many Voices
P O Box 2639
Cincinnati, OH 45201-2639

Another excellent source of identification that uses almost exclusively survivors' material is a publication called MPD Reaching Out. Often the material is presented in its raw form, handwriting changes and all. It's very nicely done. A year's subscription is $18.00.
MPD Reaching Out
c/o Public Relations Department
Royal Ottawa Hospital
1145 Carling Avenue
Ottawa, Ontario
Canada K1Z 7K4

BEYOND SURVIVAL MAGAZINE often has articles relating to multiplicity. It, too, reaches beyond the pain of abuse, and into the arena of recovery. A slick, professional publication that's very nicely done. Jody Kirk, a frequent contributor, paints pictures with words that really touch your heart. I recommend this one highly.
Beyond Survival
1278 Glenneyre St. #3
Laguna Beach, CA 92651

OTHER INCEST SURVIVOR'S MAGAZINES AND NEWSLETTERS INCLUDE:

Incest Survivor's Information Exchange (ISIE)
P O Box 3399
New Haven, CT 06515

For Crying Out Loud
Survivor's Newsletter Collective
Women's Center
46 Pleasant St.
Cambridge, MA 02139

The "Looking Up" Times
and The Survivor Resource Chronicle
Looking Up
P O Box K
Augusta, ME 04332

Survivorship
A Newsletter for Ritual Abuse Survivors
3181 Mission #139
San Francisco, CA 94110

ORGANIZATIONS

VOICES IN ACTION, INC is a self-help network for survivors and those who care about them. In addition to a regular newsletter and yearly conference, VOICES provides special interest groups, which are letter-writing groups for particular situations, including multiple personalities. Membership runs about $30.00 per year.

VOICES In Action, Inc.
P O Box 148309
Chicago, IL 60614

PARENTS UNITED often has support groups for adults molested as children. However, oftentimes these groups are in conjunction with perpetrators, and some survivors find that a little hard to swallow. Check this out with your therapist before attending. Look in the phone book or newspaper for information about local meetings.

HEALING HEARTS is an organization that deals with ritual abuse survivors and resources. They regularly sponsor workshops and training for the professional and para-professional communities.

Healing Hearts
1515 Webster St.
Oakland, CA 94612

SUPPORT GROUPS AND WORKSHOPS

Ellen Bass sometimes co-facilitates a workshop called I NEVER TOLD ANYONE with therapist Amy Pine. This three-day workshop takes place at a peaceful location in the Santa Cruz mountains in California. Using love, kindness and unconditional acceptance, Ellen and Amy help the participants deal with the abuses of their lives. (I really think Ellen is an angel in disguise.) When I completed those three days, I felt like I had done a year's worth of healing.

The last flyer I received quoted the price at $350.00 for a three-day weekend, but that includes your lodging, meals and all the love you can handle. It's worth every dime. You need to make reservations early, though, as the workshops fill up fast.

For information on the I Never Told Anyone workshops, contact:

The Survivor's Healing Center
P O Box 5296
Santa Cruz, CA 95063-5296
phone (408) 476-7174

The REACH (Restore Each Adult Child's Health) workshop is a two-day intensive psycho-drama workshop facilitated by Vic and Sue Harwood. They alternate workshops between Chicago, Illinois and Portland, Oregon. Vic, Sue and their helpers are comfortable working with multiples, and the workshop, while stressful, was most helpful. The cost is approximately $150.00 in Portland, and about $250.00 in Chicago.

For more information about a REACH workshop, contact:

Vic and Sue Harwood
7106 S.E. Harrison Street
Portland, OR 97215-4034

There are any number of 12-step groups around to deal with almost every aspect of life including alcoholism, drugs, overeating, relationships and sex, and incest. An ISA or SIA group can help lessen your feelings of isolation, and some even have groups within groups that relate to multiplicity or ritual abuse.

On the West Coast, contact:
Incest Survivors Anonymous
P O Box 5613
Long Beach, CA 90805-0613

On the East Coast, contact:
Survivors of Incest Anonymous
P. O. Box 21817
Baltimore, MD 21222-6817